Praise for

REWILDING THE HUMAN HEART

"With the flair and vivid language of a poet and the wisdom of an old soul, Sharifa Oppenheimer leads us into a deep appreciation of our relationship with self and with nature. Attuned to the spirit of the ancestors and awake to the mysteries of spirit in our time, Oppenheimer leads us on a careful examination of inner and outer nature in our own experience. This book is a trek through our inner life which we can take up if we are willing to make the effort to follow her lead. She is beckoning us to follow her into the wonder of discovery. This is a book for adults to renew the magic that children discover when their imagination is awakened in true education." —**William HS Gebel**. Astrophysicist, performing artist, psychotherapist and author, Gebel is the author of *No God or Only God, Nature's Hidden Dimension,* and *Root Speaks to Bud*

"*Rewilding the Human Heart: A Journey of Reunion* is an extraordinary guide that leads the reader into a deeply felt connection with Nature. Sharifa Oppenheimer masterfully blends scientific insights on brain development and neuroscience with humanity's elemental and evolutionary history, creating a beautiful fusion of knowledge and embodiment. Through her wisdom, the book becomes an experiential journey, inviting us to consciously engage with the seen and unseen aspects of life. Sharifa's ability to draw us into the primal forces of Earth, Water, Fire, Air, and Ether makes this an essential read for anyone seeking a deeper, more intimate relationship with the world around us—and within us. This book is a true guide for reawakening our elemental nature and becoming better stewards of our shared Earth." —**Elyshia Holliday**. Executive Director of Organization of Nature Evolutionaries (ONE)

"In *Rewilding the Human* Heart Sharifa Oppenheimer combines lyrical storytelling, keen observation and what she calls 'technologies of relationship' in order to weave the elements and their tangible expressions into an exquisite fabric of interbeing – the place where we are all connected. We are given the opportunity to not only intellectually understand this connection but to participate in practices that explore and expand our conscious awareness of our kinship with Nature where we meet in common union. This blessing of a book is like a healing balm for the wounds of separation that modernity has imposed upon us, while helping to reawaken our truly natural selves." —**Pam Montgomery**. Teacher, international speaker, founding member of United Plant Savers, and author of *Co-Creating with Nature* and *Plant Spirit Healing*

"Thank you, Sharifa, for reminding us once again that we are, at our very core, beings of mystery and wonder. The very word rewilding awakens, stirs and moves us toward awareness of the outer landscape of the elements and ether beings and, at the same time, draws us into an inner landscape that opens up a soul-deepening so needed in our time. Read *Rewilding the Human Heart* from cover to cover! Each chapter includes spirit-filled tools, teaching us to, as Sharifa says *'live in joyous co-creation with all beings.'"* —**Cynthia Aldinger**. Author of *Life is the Curriculum* and *Home Away From Home*. Founder of LifeWays North America

"In *Rewilding the Human Heart*, Sharifa invites the reader to lay down the busyness of the world to discover and deepen our primal depth of being. She guides us in an exploration of both the outward and inward aspects of the Elements: Earth, Water, Fire, Air, and Ether. Within these pages lies a lifetime of contemplations and practices for those wishing to embrace the fullness of Life. In this age, where our lives all too often keep us apart from Nature's abundant teachings, this book serves to rekindle the heritage that our ancestors knew well. Just perhaps, such a renewal will harmonize humanity with this precious planet that we have so abused." —**Wali David Via**. Pioneer and teacher of Biodynamic/Regenerative agriculture, farmer, senior teacher in the Sufi Inayatiyya Inner School, leader in the Ziraat, or Sacred Ecology movement. Importantly, he is a life-long composting devotee

"Through simple wisdom and wise exercises. Sharifa Oppenheimer invites us into deeper connection with Nature. Within this broadened kinship we learn to see ourselves and the world with fresh eyes." —**Jen Frey**. Author of *Communicating with Plants: Heart-Based Practices*, founder of Heart Springs Sanctuary, healer, mentor, earth advocate and voice of the plants.

"This work responds to a longing felt among all people, especially the youth, who are looking for some way to connect with Gaia, to find hope rather than despair or confusion amidst the state of our world. The book is rich with story and practice ~ multi-layered practices that draw one outward and inward, using the elements and realms of being as a template. Quite practical as well as poetic." —Zakira Beasley. Somatic educator and practitioner, Biodynamic cranio-sacral and poly-vagal touch therapist. Her work is informed by her Sufi and Buddhist training and many years of teaching in these traditions.

REWILDING THE HUMAN HEART

A JOURNEY OF REUNION

SHARIFA OPPENHEIMER

Red Elixir
Rhinebeck, New York

Paperback ISBN 9781966293033
eBook ISBN 9781966293040

"To Honor All Beings" reprinted from *A Litany of Wild Graces* (Red Elixir, 2022)

Book design by Colin Rolfe

Red Elixir is an imprint of Monkfish Book Publishing Company

Red Elixir
22 East Market Street, Suite 304
Rhinebeck, New York 12572
(845) 876-4861
redelixirbooks.com
monkfishpublishing.com

Acknowledgments

Of First Importance

I give thanks to the great mystery, who was once *a hidden treasure that longed to be known.* Gratitude to the One whose light illumines the universe as well as our own minds. This One Love is the force that carries swirling galaxies and births stars, which has placed my life and the lives of all beings into this shimmering sphere, the Earth.

Much gratitude to the mineral beings that form the stream bed outside my kitchen door, and to the mountain waters that sing of many moods and seasons. Gratitude to the scented pines and grace-filled tulip poplars, to the foxes that bark at dawn and the owls hunting beneath the stars. To the countless beings who teach us goodness, beauty, reciprocity, generosity, joy, persistence, forbearance, resilience, truth and so much more. They are a *living* litany of wild graces.

Now to Thank My Human Collaborators

I acknowledge and thank the Monacan Nation, the original and present keepers of the land and waters in Virginia, the place I call home. I give gratitude as well to First Nations people worldwide. They continue to hold crucial knowledge, both spiritual and scientific; they are on the front lines of protecting Earth, our only home, as well.

To Hazrat Inayat Khan for lifelong inspiration, especially his insight into the livingness of nature and breathing in communion with the elements; these are his foundational practices.

To Llewellyn Vaughan Lee for pointing me always toward the Feminine as she appears in our emerald earth.

To Atum O'Kane for his deep study of Jungian Alchemy and his embodied transmission of this wisdom.

To Elyshia Holliday and the *Organization of Nature Evolutionaries* for partnering with me to share the material in this book as a course through their online offerings.

To Acacia Moore and *LifeWays North America* for, again, partnering with me to make this material available as a course for parents and families through their online offerings.

To Moinuddin Christopher Clarke for diving deeply into the manuscript and offering elegant insights that broaden the view.

To my many friends who read, questioned, commented and helped me polish this till it glows.

To my hero and amazing husband Eric for listening, reading, editing, offering necessary advice, as well as caring for me during the many months I was immobilized on the couch ~ healing a broken ankle ~ as I wrote this book.

Join Sharifa online as she leads the practices in this book.
Breathwork, Guided Meditations,
Gratitude Bundles and Elemental Altars

https://www.sharifaoppenheimer.org/
rewilding-the-human-heart-meditations

They will open your heart
to a fully embodied relationship
with the Elements and Realms of Nature.
See you there!

Contents

Introduction

REWILDING THE HUMAN *Heart* is a celebration of new ways to honor our earth-ancestors and deepen these primal relationships. As we dive into the cardinal elements of Earth, Water, Fire, Air and Ether, as well as nature's realms ~ Minerals, Plants, Animals, Humans and Unseen Beings ~ we also rekindle their wild and essential nature within our own being. In this way we become better relatives to our fellow earthlings.

Chapter by chapter we become immersed in the components of our luminous *biosphere*. We deepen our felt experience of the elements and invite the realms of nature into closer relationship. Because we are composed of these very elements and realms, we will discover how their qualities, moods, gifts and challenges exist within our luminous *inner sphere*. We will deepen into relationship with these earth-ancestors on many levels, within our body, heart, soul, mind, and spirit. Their wildness will rekindle our own wild and tender wisdom.

Each chapter incorporates an array of tools ~ technologies of relationship ~ that foster an embodied exploration. These "technologies" allow our awareness to sink down from the inquiring mind and settle more deeply into the regions of our sensitive heart, our eternal soul, and the *soft animal of our body*, thereby engaging the wholeness of being human.[1]

Technologies of Relationship

Over the millennia humans have learned tangible ways of fostering relationship with each other and the more-than-human world. Our lives were spent observing the myriad ways plants, insects, birds, and other animals communicate. The gifts of song, movement, breath and blessing are lessons humans have learned from our other-than-human kin. I call these ways of communicating *technologies of relationship*. We will employ these technologies ~ these embodied languages ~ within our deepening kinship with nature.

Song is earth's first language, articulated by wind in treetops; by water rushing over stones and dropping into clear pools; by birdsong at dawn, autumn crickets, geese flying in formation; by coyote whom we call the song dog and vixen's song of love. Like our ancient ancestors around the fire at the cave's edge, we too can discover the magic of song as we embed ourselves more deeply into our own immediate pocket of the emerald earth. As we walk our favorite trail or sit in the twilit back yard, allow song to arise from your listening heart. Offer this simple song as a gift to these other-than-human relatives who surround you.

Movement, like song, is a primal language spoken by countless beings. Certainly, we speak through movement too. Neuroscience, as well as our own experience, shows that rhythmic, continuous movement soothes the soul. Outer harmonious movements bring harmony to interior body rhythms; here we find comfort and rest. Dance has spoken volumes since the dawn of creation. Think of the bird-of-paradise's elegant courting dance or the playful grooming, chasing, bumping and tumbling of coyote mates. David Abram, the celebrated cultural ecologist and geophilosopher, encourages us to dance with the wild, a depth ecology movement and arts practice which he calls Place Dancing. As we settle more deeply into relationship with our earth-elders, let's playfully move the way they do. Stand up and allow the breezes to ruffle your hair, spread your wings and feel the lift of wind, feel that your bones are filled with air.

Breath is a more subtle form of earth-language. The forest breathes as breezes ruffle treetops. The small creek outside my door breathes with the movements of the water. Prairie grasses breathe in wind sliding down mountainsides, while prairie voles, most affectionate of mates, snuggle side by side and breathe in unison. Human rituals bring us together in song, dance, and unified breath: think of the rhythmic breathing of ritual's call and response. We can deepen our kinship with the natural world through breathing in unison with Gaia's children. Stand beside the sea to breathe with her waves or observe her longer breath cycles of high and low tides. Step outdoors and breathe with the oaks on a windy night.

Blessing is another subtle form of communication, another intrinsic technology of relationship. Blessing is so ubiquitous ~ it is everywhere in nature ~ that to us it can easily go unnoticed. Trees exude medicinal particulates that lower stress levels; soil organisms offer us happiness; honey bees make an excess of honey in order to share; dolphins protect human swimmers, honey-guide birds direct humans to honey trees.... the list goes on. We can bring blessing into our daily communion with nature by simply being aware of our footsteps. Press blessing down into the soft loam and breathe blessing into the clear blue sky.

Story is one of the ways human beings have developed technologies of relationship that are suited specifically to our own needs and talents. Our more finely articulated language capacity, located in the frontal lobes of the brain (the thinking brain) give rise to humanity's long and honored tradition of Storytelling. Here is David Abram on storytelling: "Spoken stories were the living encyclopedias of our oral ancestors. Tales told on special occasions carried the secrets of how to orient in the local cosmos. Hidden in the magic adventures of their characters were precise instructions for the hunting of various animals and for enacting the appropriate rituals of respect and gratitude, as well as specific insight regarding which plants were food and which were poison. They told us how to prepare herbs for cramps, sleeplessness or fever. The stories carried instructions that taught, more generally, how to live well in this land, without destroying its wild vitality."

A good way to get to know a new neighbor, or to deepen the acquaintance is to ask about their beginnings, to hear their stories. As we explore kinship with nature we can gain insight into our earth-kin by discovering stories that have been handed down through the generations.

Each chapter of *Rewilding the Human Heart* engages us with stories, poems, earth sciences and psychological explorations. At the end of each chapter, I offer you *Deepening Practices* to bring the lessons home, to help them embed not simply in the mind, but to resonate in your feeling heart and live in your body's memory, the geography of your cellular structure. It is when you engage emotionally and bodily with the activities described below that the magic of song, movement, breath and blessing will unfurl in your life. As you engage in these embodied ways, you are also calling on the ancient alchemy of Story. You will be writing a fresh chapter, full of earth wisdom, not only into your own personal story but also into the evolving love-story of earth's evolution.

Deepening Practices

These *Deepening Practices* are designed to bring understanding through various learning modalities:

- *Action* is the way our *body* understands life, and therefore learns <u>what to do.</u>
- *Images* are the way our *heart* understands emotion and therefore learns <u>how to feel.</u>
- *Thought* is the way our *mind* understands (both analyzing and synthesizing experiences) and therefore learns <u>how to respond</u> to life.

It is through the braiding together of action, images and thought that we can more fully participate in life's unfolding within this green world. These multidimensional ways of knowing help us come more intimately into kinship with the countless beings who compose the living body of our Mother Earth. Chapter by chapter we interact with each of these earth-cousins, engaging in rituals, stories and concepts.

Action ~ Rituals are bodily *actions* that are attended to with consciousness, intention, rhythm and repetition; this imbues our movements with natural power. Through this innate power we are connected with a greater whole, a greater being. Ritual is an important way our body thinks; the conscious, rhythmic activities carry us beyond our "little self." This is how the body gleans meaning from the ocean of sensory experiences through which we swim every day and throughout a life. Here I offer you rituals to do at home, to feel into and explore:

*Create an indoor or outdoor Honoring Place, an altar you will slowly build to honor the Elements and Realms.

*Create Gratitude Bundles, which you will give away as gifts of nourishment to our fellow earthlings.

Images are the foundation of Storytelling ~ They arise from both our own interior experience, as well as those offered us through works of art. The crucial element we need to remember is that Story, with all its rich imagery, is an intuitive way the human heart thinks. It is the way our heart understands emotion, and therefore we learn how to be human. Each chapter will begin with a story that relates to the element or realm we are studying. It is a colorful thread in the tapestry of your understanding. These stories act as catalysts, seeding your own imagination and dreamscapes. This creative imagination spills over as you work with images through artistic means. In each chapter you will:

*Create a Kinship Collage: images speak to a deeper aspect of our self than the mind. We will create a "collage-story" of images for each chapter. These images will represent the material we have explored.

Thought ~ Through weaving together the activities we engage with ritual, and through the images we encounter with story and collage, we begin to create the fabric of thought. Thought gives us perspective; it allows us to step back from the moment-by-moment sensory and emotional banquet. In this way we discover the organic patterns of our life. The recognition of these patterns allows us to see the whole picture in its totality. It is the sensorial activities of ritual and the palpable images of story that keep thought tethered to the living breathing reality that we call Gaia.

In each chapter, after the introductory story, we will dive into the realm of concept and thought. We will engage the mind, understanding that what we consider to be our own mind is a holon of the universal mind.[2] We'll explore the Element and corollary Realm ~ Minerals, Plants, Animals, Humans and Unseen Beings ~ with a look into science, finding their place in the outer landscape. We will also explore our relationship to these fellow earthlings, as well as the responsibilities entailed. We then journey toward the Element and Realm in the inner landscape, the landscape of the soul. We'll discover its place in our transforming, unfolding psyche and self. Studying ways to engage the Element and Realm, always looking toward dynamic balance, we consciously participate in the transformation of our soul. To weave together the threads of these soul journeys we will:

*Create a *Rewilding Human Nature* Journal: In each chapter you'll find Questions for Inner Inquiry and Guided Imagery experiences. I encourage you to engage with these questions and guided meditations. Have inner conversations with different aspects of yourself and listen for their answers. Choose a beautiful journal, or perhaps you'd prefer a larger sketch pad. In this journal you can record your musings, the replies you hear, perhaps write a poem. A sketch book gives you the opportunity to render your thoughts in images, and to use it for collage-making as well.

I am excited to step into this Journey of Reunion with you. Let's begin.

CHAPTER ONE

The Earth Element and Mineral Realm

Sacred Earth ~ Stardust

IN THIS CHAPTER we explore the grounding, steadying influence of the Earth Element. We discover ways to find earth as a touchstone in our daily lives, as well as ways to honor our Mother in the natural world. We also live into the foundational nature of minerals ~ within our own bones and bloodstream, as well as in the world of the Stone People.

Let's begin this journey into the depths of Earth and Minerals in the way of our ancestors. Let's engage some original technologies of relationship: now we begin with *Story*. This is my retelling of the tale of Sky Woman Falling, as told by Robin Wall Kimmerer in her ground-breaking book *Braiding Sweetgrass*.[3] After listening, we will *Breathe in communion with Earth*.[4]

SKY WOMAN FALLING

In the beginning there was the Skyworld. Sky Woman awoke one morning and as usual began her day with a walk through the dawn's light. She carried a small pouch; into this she placed berries she found and seeds of the beloved plants she met along the way. She stopped beneath her favorite tree to sit among its roots nibbling on berries. As she sat listening to the bird's morning chorale, she gazed at the wonders gathered all about her. She sat quietly admiring the strength and steadiness of the roots she was nestled among.

It was then that she noticed a crack between the roots. She had never seen this before. How could she have missed it? She bent a bit closer to get a better look, but she could not see the bottom of this crack. Now, she knelt beside the crack and put her face very close, peering into a darkness she had never encountered. She leaned a bit further, to see better...that was when she lost her balance and fell.

Sky Woman came swirling down, cosmic clouds whirled about her like a silken cloak. She fell for a very long time, clutching her pouch close to her heart.

As she looked around, she saw only dark water far below, so very different than her home in the world of light.

Down below, though, there were many eyes gazing at…what could that be? They saw only a small creature spiraling ever closer. Finally, as she came close, they saw this was a woman. It was the geese who had been watching her descent. They commented to one another, "She does not have feathers and wings; she cannot fly above the water!" "She has no fins or gills, to live within the water." "She will not survive; let us help her!"

With one motion, the geese arose honking and calling to let her know help was on the way. They flew close together, that they might catch her with their soft-feathered wings. Gently they carried her down. Now, other people ~ water-people ~ had been watching her descent as well. Loons, beavers, otters and many fish began to confer. How could they be of any help? A great turtle offered his large shell, and when the geese arrived, she stepped off their strong wings onto the patterned turtle shell.

The water people knew very well that she was not equipped for a life in the deeps; they knew she needed land to make a life upon. The deep-divers had heard, in old tales told by grandparents, that there was something called mud at the bottom of the water. Perhaps this would suffice. They agreed to find this mysterious mud for their new guest.

Loon, such a strong swimmer, made the deep dive first. But the distance down was too far; he arrived back empty-handed. Others now offered to help: Sturgeon, Beaver, Otter all dove as deeply as they could, but to no avail. Others tried their skill till finally only little Muskrat was left. He said "I will go, I will do my very best!" The others knew Muskrat was small and the weakest diver of them all. But he insisted and began the long downward journey. He was gone a very long time.

Everyone waited, hoping for the safe return of their small relative. Finally bubbles began to arise. But with them, the small limp body of Muskrat arose too. He had given his life to help this human woman, so in need of earth. His cousins mourned his loss, till someone noticed that clutched in his paw was the mud they had all sought.

Giving Sky Woman this mud, she spread it on the back of the great turtle. Now, in gratitude for the generosity of all the animals, especially Muskrat, she began to sing and dance upon the great turtle's back. As she danced, the mud *expanded and soon the whole world was created from the gift of mud the animals had given.*

Sky Woman now realized that she still held her pouch, which contained the seeds of so many of her most beloved plants from Sky World. She walked through the newly-made earth, scattering seeds wherever she went. She cared for and tended these seeds, just the way she had been taught when she was a girl. Sunlight streamed down from her old home and soon the entire earth was green, flourishing abundantly. Food plants and medicine plants grew, tall trees provided shade and fruiting bushes offered sweets. With such a banquet of generosity from the plants, animals began to arrive. This, my friends, is how we all came to live together on Turtle Island.

BREATHE WITH EARTH

Let's sit and hold the images of this story, as we breathe in unison with Mother Earth. Let us greet Earth with honor:[5]

Beloved Mother Earth, I greet you with Gratitude and Love.
  Your steady earth is sacred; I walk on holy ground,
  Your abundance inspires my generosity,
  I live in accord with your healing rhythms.
  Your enfolding presence holds me, centered in love.
I give you honor and praise.

- Sit comfortably and relax, breathing in and out through the nose.
- Enjoy a few breaths and relax into the rhythm.
- Become aware of the stability of earth beneath you. Feel the energy move in and out through your feet or the bottom of your spine.
- As you exhale allow any tension or density to be pulled downward and drawn into the living soil; the spirit of the soil bacteria will regenerate this energy as compost.
- As you inhale be aware of the revitalizing, fresh magnetic energy of earth pulsing up through your feet, into your spine. Feel green leaves budding from your skin.

- Stay with this cycling, steadying earth energy moving through you for as long as you like.
- End with a deep bow of gratitude.

Earth in the Outer Landscape ~ Earth as a Gift from the Stars
Sacred Earth

In the Potawatomi story of Sky Woman spiraling down from above, we see a common theme in origin stories worldwide: many tell of life on earth being given as a gift, whirling toward us from the stars. One of ancient India's origin stories tells us life began as white swirls in a sea of milk. The Greek myth of the goddess Gaia portrays her as spinning out of darkness, wrapped in flowing white veils. [6]

Photos from the Webb telescope show us our current origin story. We see the same swirling forms as our ancient ancestors, but we now name

them protogalaxies. They whirl and dance in space long before planets form, long before evolution can occur. These swirling gasses became liquid under the pressure of the galactic whirlpool. Hot liquid touches cold space and earth's crust is formed, like a crust on pudding. Rocks were formed by the crusts melting and cooling over eons. Slowly, slowly, with volcanic action bringing new molten lava to the surface, mountains arose and our earth became shaped.

We can think of all life on earth as born from stones, from rock and mineral rearranging itself over billions of years. Everything on our earth came to be, originating from this rocky mineral mantle. We arose from these star-born gifts; minerals are the foundation that brings all life to the point we find ourselves today.

Life is self-creating and self-maintaining. Gaia is a unified conscious, intelligent Being. She is a *holon* within the *holarchy* of the cosmos. A holon is a whole being, nested within interconnecting larger beings. How does this work? It is the nature of Life to incorporate smaller wholes into larger ones, thus creating ever greater complexity and diversity. Here is a familiar simple example: Electrons and protons gather to become atoms, atoms constellate to become molecules; molecules coalesce to become cells; cells collaborate to constitute organs; organs cooperate in infinite ways to become our own bodies. We gather together into families and communities; humanity is held within the unity that is nature; nature ~ including human nature ~ composes the living being that is earth. We are a series of holons nesting within ever-greater holons, held with the holarchy of the cosmos.

Earth operates in constant transformation and is the protector of essential life and death cycles. She is a vast composting system: forests, prairies, waters, oceans, migrating animals that deposit nutrients in rhythmic cycles, bodies dying, composting, decomposing and recomposing. Death is essential to the fertile womb that births new life. This is how *Life creates the conditions necessary for life.*

From the level of cells and molecules to ancient matriarchal societies, *Gaia's fundamental principles* are abundance, generosity, relationship, distribution on the basis of need, not merit, cooperation and collaboration, gratitude and celebration. These Gaian principles reigned for millennia, but in humanity's recent past they have been abandoned for free-market principles that go against life's fundamental structure. This endangers all living systems and beings. We need only know that due to the ever-increasing use of chemical fertilizers and pesticides as well as the quickening pace of desertification, in 2021 the UN projected that we have sixty harvests left before earth's soil is completely depleted. Yet, solutions *do* exist and year by year we are hurrying to employ them. Consider the healing capacities of regenerative agriculture, water-catchment systems, urban gardens, eating in-season, community supported agriculture farms, BIPOC food sovereignty movements and more. Each action we make, when it arises not from fear or anger, rather from the depth of our loving heart, resonates with the abundant life-giving heart of Gaia.

Earth in the Inner Landscape: Alchemy and the Transformation of Self

The Earth Element in the inner landscape mirrors earth in the exterior.[7]

We carry earth within ourselves. When the Earth Element is balanced in our soul, we discover earth in the qualities of rhythm, stability, security, simplicity, confidence and equanimity. We even employ egalitarian distribution of energy when we honor the needs of the body and emotions equally with the mind. We also carry within our cells the blueprint of transformative cycles: we live through cycles of germinating, growing, blossoming, fruiting, seeding and decay. As in the physical functioning of earth, in which death and decay are crucial to new life, also in the inner landscape we must engage in composing and decomposing aspects of the self. Rudolf Steiner, Austrian philosopher and father of Waldorf Education, speaks of the seven-year cycles through which the human being grows. As we move through these developmental stages, he insists we must let go of the old to make way for the new.

We also carry earth within ourselves in the ability to *manifest* our soul's dreams, to discover our purpose in this world and step by step bring this purpose into life. We have come to earth like Sky Woman, falling from the stars and bringing seeds ~ our unique gifts ~ to offer. Let us discover this purpose and step forward bringing these seeds to our fellow earthlings.

But, you ask, how do we consciously bring our soul-dreams into manifestation? To accomplish this, we need five things:

a. *Commitment:* Intention is everything. Once committed, *Do Not Waver.* Simply turn the mind and heart back in the direction you are going. When challenges arise, don't question your commitment, instead investigate ways to accommodate these challenges. Be like the river moving around boulders.

b. *Time:* Make accommodations in our daily, weekly, and seasonal schedule. Evaluate how we use our time; eliminate the wasted time: social media? shopping as entertainment? chasing after daydreams?

c. *Space:* Clear out our physical, emotional, and mental spaces. This aspect of clearing out physical space is crucial: Goodwill is your friend. This makes room for whatever the physical manifestation of your dream requires. If emotional baggage holds you back, get the help you need: think of therapy or life-coaching. If your mind is cluttered with daily headlines and marketing rabbit-holes, ration your on-line time.

d. *Form:* What is the right context, within what relationships will this soul-dream thrive? Discover who your collaborators are, where and how your dream can come to earth.

e. *Action:* You have committed, made time available, cleared space and recognized the context ~ the form. Now is the time to make the plan real. What is the first step? Begin with three "first steps." Listen inwardly and outwardly; read the signs. Know that it is the light of your soul that makes the path visible as you proceed. You do not need to see the entirety of the path laid out before you begin; rather pay attention to each step and listen for whispers of inspiration.

Earth qualities also give us the capacity to *Hold the Center,* to find ground in the midst of uncertainty. We live with vast earth transformations occurring about us: we walk into a future where the old maps are obsolete. We must discover new-and-ancient ways; we must leave way-markers for those to come. In these times of unimaginable horrors and breath-taking beauty, how do we hold the center? We, again, look to Earth as our teacher:

Hold the Center in Daily Rhythms: We give attention to the care of body through regularity in sleeping and waking, eating and drinking, in physical activity and rest, in work and play. It is also crucial that we balance time indoors with plenty of time in the revivifying rhythms of nature.

We give attention to the care of the emotions through regular deep connection with our beloved family and friends. We mammals, and especially humans, are designed to thrive within intimate circles of those we love. We, in fact, are deeply influenced ~ we could say we are shaped ~ by those with whom we are closest.

We give attention to the care of the soul by discovering what activities bring us quiet joy and peace. What invigorates and inspires us? A walk in the woods? Gardening? Prayer? Song? Dance? Art?

We give attention to the care of the spirit through a meditative practice. Look in the Appendix for a simple eyes-open heart-breathing meditation. This can be done anywhere, especially as a walking meditation. The best part? No one can tell you are meditating: you nod, smile, say a few words, gather them into your vast, peaceful heart and continue consciously breathing.

Hold the Center in Seasonal Rhythms: Give attention to Earth's cycles and to the moods of the season. Notice your interior response. Humans evolved by being held in the arms of Mother Nature. Her rhythms are printed deeply into our DNA. Even in our twenty-first century lives, in which we may have consciously forgotten these life-affirming rhythms, they continue to resonate within. Honor these large yearly rhythms, and feel our body, emotions, and minds settle into ancient and familiar cycles. When we correlate our actions to the flow of the seasons it gives these actions great power of fulfillment.

Springtime: Go outdoors as soon as you feel the seeds rolling over in their underground beds. Day by day be aware of the staccato rhythm of springtime's arrival: two warm days, then perhaps a light frost. Bring your whole self out into spring's tentative steps and feel these moods as they pass through your cells. Become the new growth of spring.

Summer: Don't hide indoors cocooned in the cold mausoleum of air conditioning. Take off as many clothes as is legal, put on a big floppy hat and go out into the heat, the humidity that presses down on all sides. Feel the trickle of sweat down your neck, cooling as it slides down your spine. Notice as your animal senses seek shade and water. Become a hippo nearly submerged in your local pool. Relax into deep heat and warm water; relax into your warm animal body.

Autumn: Let your senses run wild as you rake leaf piles. Jump in them with your children, and grandchildren, or any children, laugh and scramble out. Repeat often. Pick-your-own apples and be immersed in the sweet aroma of applesauce simmering. Pick a pumpkin and bake a pie. Join your infinite ancestors in autumn's abundant gifts. Sing and dance in gratitude for such generosity.

Winter: Sink into this interior time; Mother Earth is resting, incubating seeds in warmth and quiet. Follow suit: lay some of your projects aside, build a fire in your back yard on a sunny cold day. Sit close as you gaze into the flames and poke the coals with a stick. Look for bird footprints in the snow beneath the birdfeeder. Go to bed early and notice your winter dreams. Rest and wait for your internal seeds to germinate in your quiet underground interior.

The way we Hold the Center is by holding each aspect of our self in the center of the One Heart. We can arrive in the center of our own heart by attending to these earthly rhythms. It is here, at home in the heart, that we find we are also in the center of the great heart of Gaia, in the center of the vast Cosmos, in the center of the One Being.

We may also find challenging earth qualities ~ when earth is not in balance within our self. Perhaps we have a tendency to hold on too tightly. Hold on to our own ideas, our answers, our world views. Letting go must be the balance to holding on, and finding discernment in the midst of these seemingly opposing forces can be difficult. Another challenge of imbalanced earth is a sluggishness, feeling thick-headed, or a sense of walking through molasses. "Stuck in our own ways," "An old stick-in-the-mud," these are common expressions of imbalanced earth qualities. Imbalanced earth can arrive as dogmatism, as well: a sense that our answers are the right ones and everyone else should just admit it and do as we do. Stiff-necked, in other words.

We can practice and deepen relationship to Earth in simple, powerful ways. At some point during each day take an "earth break." Go outdoors, take off your shoes and simply feel the subtle electromagnetic energy of the earth moving up through your body. Consciously breathe this potent, purifying energy. Let the earth draw down anything you need to let go. Become a tree, pulling the nutrients up through your whole self. Walk, slowly breathing through your feet.

Not good weather? Lie down on the floor in front of a chair or couch. Stretch your spine its full length, put your bottom against the legs of the chair or couch, with knees and legs supported by the seat. Relax, relax, relax. Feel yourself sinking down into the soft loam of earth, being entirely held by earth. Breathe in unison with our mother.

INQUIRY QUESTIONS FOR THE INNER LANDSCAPE

a. How has my life supported my soul's journey; remember how Sky Woman's geese supported her.

b. What challenges have I encountered? How have I met these challenges? How have I forged my own way, led by the light of my soul?

c. What soul dream have I brought into the world: What deep soul desire have I manifested?

d. Do I have a new dream-seed that wants to be planted? What will manifesting it entail? What commitment, time, space, form and action are necessary?

e. Is there anything in myself that is too stuck, too stubborn, too sclerosed? What needs to be buried and therefore decompose in order to become rich soil for the new?

Minerals in the Biosphere

It is an astonishing fact that forty thousand metric tons of stardust fall on earth each year. What an inspiration to be aware that we are breathing micro-fragments of stars directly into our being, at all times. We think of young children as coming to earth with stars in their eyes; what would it be like if we knew that we, as well, walk through life with stars gleaming from within us? What would happen if we understood that each human and more-than-human being carries the wisdom of the stars? Stop for a moment and just imagine....

Gaia's deep-time story begins with these cosmic minerals coalescing throughout time-beyond-time and forming a rocky mantle around her molten core. These minerals come to us from the cosmos, they carry the light of the stars, and we can even see starlight in their glitter. Think particularly of flint whose magical spark is made of light. The unique electromagnetic signature of each mineral carries the story, or perhaps a many-layered story of its lives as a star. It is true to say that all earth-life has evolved from mineral transformations, and all earth life continues to depend upon minerals.

All sea life depends upon minerals, as well. The most important property of seawater is the concentration of its dissolved nutrients; most critical of these are the minerals nitrogen and phosphorus. Salt water is carried by ocean currents to Antarctica. Liquids expand when frozen, so the freezing temperatures squeeze out salt and other minerals. Because these minerals are heavier, they drop down below the ice where circulating currents carry these to warm, shallow coastal waters. Here, phytoplankton proliferate so exuberantly, so generously that these plant plankton blooms can be seen from space. Satellite images show us these vast bright green colonies feathering out along continental coastlines especially in the tropics and far beyond. Zooplankton, microscopic organisms, feast on this and flourish. These blooms thus form the bottom of the marine food chain. Calcium and carbonate, two other minerals contained in seawater, form the basis of marine animal's skeletons and shells.

All plant life on land depends upon at least fourteen mineral elements for their nutrition. Potassium and magnesium are particularly essential minerals, as they are necessary to the process of photosynthesis. All animals' bones, including our own, are composed of the minerals calcium and phosphorus. These provide the bones with a hard framework and combine with the protein collagen which offers pliability. This combination of collagen and minerals makes bone alive and strong, flexible enough to withstand stress. Minerals are crucial to health and well-being in other ways as well; they influence muscle and nerve function and regulate the body's water balance. Electrolytes, which are essential minerals, flow through our blood and other body fluids; they are vital for basic life functioning.

Given the pivotal role minerals play in the biosphere, let's explore ways to enliven our awareness and deepen our relationship with them in our inner lives.

How to Consciously Make Relationship with Minerals in the Inner Spheres
We Are Stardust

Perhaps you already have a budding relationship with Mineral Beings. Sometimes minerals call to us in dreams. Have your dreams been graced by rose quartz? by tourmaline? by jade or sapphire? Are you attracted to particular minerals? Perhaps you know minerals as healers and are aware of the healing properties of stones. Homeopathic medicine often invites minerals as allies in their remedies, and Anthroposophic medicine offers, among other minerals, the remedy meteoric iron when courage and impetus are needed.

Let's begin to make relationship with the Mineral Realm through a visualization practice. We carry the minerality of the stars in our blood stream and other life processes, but our most palpable experience of them is in our bones. Let us greet the Mineral Beings:

> *Beloved Stone Beings,*
> *Your stardust flows through my veins,*
> *Your nutrients nourish my body.*
> *Your beauty inspires my soul.*
> *Through You, I am a mountain walking.*
> *I give you gratitude and love.*

VISUALIZE OUR MINERALITY
- So, let us settle into our body. Allow our awareness to drift down from the head and settle more deeply into the region of the heart.
- Allow the breath to swing through the heart; you may feel that you are a child again, swinging from a long rope on the

branch of a tree in your back yard. Or perhaps you have an ancient memory of being rocked in a cradle.

- Be aware, in this movement, of how your bones give you the structure to remain intact, yet they are pliable enough to allow exquisite whole-body movements: the exhilaration of the swing or the hypnotic rocking of the cradle.
- Stay with this healing rhythm, remaining aware of the way bones offer us stability-within-movement.
- Now turn your attention to the minerality of your spine. Feel this stability arising from the base of your spine. Become aware of your bones branching into your rib cage, your limbs, your bony skull crowning all.
- Feel how all your flesh and soft parts mold so beautifully around these sturdy bones. Feel as though you could sit here ~ forever stable, yet with body rhythms forever in motion. Entirely in balance.
- Feel kinship with the mountains; perhaps you have a favorite mountain. Breathe this slow, certain mountain-breath.
- Now become aware of both yourself-as-mountain, as well as yourself walking the mountain's forest path. Allow your senses to open and become alive.
- Feel the breeze brush your arm, the warm sun caresses your cheek, listen to birdsong and your own footfall as leaves crunch, smell the tang of pine pitch, and leaf mold.
- Now you turn a bend in the path; what surprise do you find here? A favorite stone glittering in the path? A smooth boulder beckoning you? A tumble of stones asking to be stacked as a cairn?
- Sit beside your Mineral Being, or lie down on its warm smoothness, or hold it in your hand and caress it.
- Greet this being as a member of the Stone People, our most ancient ancestors. Give honor and gratitude. Allow your bones to speak to the bones of the earth. Merge with this Mineral Being; yourself, this Stone Being, and the mountain ~ We are ONE.
- Stay with this stable union as long as you like.

    — When you stand to return to your day ~ Walk Like A Mountain!

Questions to Deepen Your Relationship with the Mineral Realm

If you can, visit your favorite stone or boulder. You might also hold this member of the Stone People Nation in your hand or visit them in meditation.

    — breathe in unison with your Stone Being

    — with respect ask these questions:

        What does it *feel like* to be you?

        What gift do you bring to me now?

        What do you need from me in return?

End with several breaths. *Offer Blessing to Earth and Minerals.* Commit to explore your relationship with minerals more fully as you move through your days.

DEEPENING PRACTICES FOR CHAPTER ONE

Deepening Practices are designed to help you live more fully into your connection with the Elements and Realms of Nature. Each chapter you will be creating and slowly building a sacred place to honor and connect with the particular element and realm. You will also learn to make a gratitude offering, to nourish your relationship with the beings of nature. As we move through the journey of these chapters you are invited to collect images of each Element and Realm to create either a single collage for that chapter, or perhaps a unifying collage near the completion. In this same way, your journal will be a map of your journey that you can refer to in the future.

    Remember Ritual: As we discussed in the introduction, ritual is a deeply human practice that can teach us via three modalities: *Action, Images,* and *Thought. Action* is the way our *body* understands life. Our bodies are designed to learn through action, and therefore we learn <u>what to do</u>. *Images* are the way our *heart* understands emotion and therefore we learn <u>how to feel</u>. *Thought* is the way our *mind* understands (both analyzing and synthesizing experiences) and therefore we learn <u>how to respond</u> to life. When we employ all three ways of learning, these offer gratitude and blessings to Earth and Minerals. We will be cultivating all these, as we engage in our deepening practices.

As time allows, choose one of these activities or, perhaps best, engage with all:

- In the realm of *Action*, you are invited to give care and attention to creating an Honoring Space and a Gratitude Bundle.
- In the realm of *Images* you are invited to give loving imagination to creating a Kinship Collage.
- In the realm of *Thought* you are invited to mindfully attend to your internal inquiries through writing in your Journal.

PLACE FOR HONORING THE REALMS: OUTDOOR SIT-SPOT OR INDOOR NATURE SPACE

Let's begin by choosing where we will build this Honoring-Place for the Realms; let's find the right place for it to live and evolve ~ indoors or out ~ throughout this journey. This space can be an indoor place or a sit-spot outside. If you are indoors, choose a beautiful cloth to define the space. If outdoors, gather small stones, branches or other materials to delineate sacred space.

We will bring Earth and Minerals as a foundation. You might gather a handful of living soil, place it in a small bowl and set it in the midst of stones and crystals that you find, or ones you have collected. With attention and respect, place these earth-cousins on your altar.

Each day go to your sacred place to greet the Earth and Minerals; give honor and thanks for the qualities of life force and steadiness. Now is the time, more than ever, to ground into the sustenance, safety, deep nourishment, and sense of stability that the Earth provides. Be aware, also, of the gift of ancient stars; see their distant light glitter here in the minerals before you. For a moment, feel the stardust falling all about you. Bow and smile.

CREATE A GRATITUDE BUNDLE FOR THE EARTH ELEMENT AND REALM OF MINERALS

With each step we take, our footfall lands on Sacred Ground; we are healed by Earth's steady, rhythmic electromagnetic field. Minerals live within our very bones and bloodstream. These star-born minerals are the genesis of life on Earth, and millennia later they continue to nourish all ~ microbes, plants, animals, and humans. It is our gift and responsibility to give honor and gratitude; we do this by offering "Earth Prayers," our gratitude bundles. In this way, we nourish the Element of Earth and the Realm of Minerals.

+ You can begin with either a piece of paper or a large leaf. If you choose paper, paint or color an image that represents the Earth Element and Realm of Minerals. Or, if you prefer, you can write a poem or a few lines of thanks and offerings.
+ Now gather the items that go inside your paper or leaf, for the offering package. When I do this, I usually choose seed, root, stem, flower, leaf, and fruit. But the offering is yours to make, so you choose what you feel represents your gratitude best.
   o Now you will fold the paper or leaf in a way that honors earth, sky, generosity and encircling protection.
   o Fold from the bottom a third of the way up; this reminds us of gratitude to Mother Earth.
   o Next, fold from the top down a third of the way; this reminds us of gratitude to Father Sky.
   o Now, fold from the left a third of the way across; this reminds us of gratitude to the feminine principle of generosity in our daily life.
   o Finally, fold from the right a third of the way across; this reminds us of gratitude to the masculine principle of enfolding protection in our daily life.

- Tie the bundle with a long piece of grass or a string made of natural materials.
- Take your bundle outdoors to your "sacred spot." With prayer, song and ritual, plant your offering as a seed of gratitude. In this way, we nourish the Element of Earth and the Realm of Minerals.

Create your own prayer, or use the following as a springboard. Make your prayer audible ~ speak or sing ~ as you give the offering:

Beloved Star-born Stone People, you are our most primal relatives. You continue to nourish and heal us. All of Mother Earth's bounty is held steady and secure by you. We give you honor, gratitude and love. Please accept this prayer bundle from my deep heart.

KINSHIP COLLAGE

Peruse old National Geographics and other nature magazines or print images from the internet that represent the Earth Element and the Mineral Realm. Gather these into a folder. As you finish this chapter, you can create an Earth Element and Mineral Realm collage. Or perhaps you'd rather wait to the end of your journey through this course and create a collage of all the elements and realms unified into a single multidimensional image. You can begin to cut, shape, paint, color, calligraph, and create a collage that integrates all these earth beings into the unified whole that we experience here on our green Earth!

REWILDING HUMAN NATURE JOURNAL

In this chapter you find *Questions for Inner Inquiry* into your relationship with Earth, as well as practices to deepen your kinship with Minerals. I encourage you to consider these questions, have inner conversations with different aspects of yourself and listen for their answers. Use your journal or larger sketch pad. Write your musings, the replies you hear, perhaps write a poem. Render your thoughts in images; you can use these for collage-making as well.

CHAPTER TWO

The Water Element and Plant Realm

Waters of Life ~ The World Tree

Now we turn toward the essential nature of Water and her life-giving qualities of purification, revivification, accommodation, flow and connection. We explore the magic of water within the living systems of earth and within our own bodies and souls. We inquire how to foster a balanced water element both within and without.

We also explore the Realm of Plants: recognizing plants as integral participants in Earth's hydrologic cycle and as the creators of the air we breathe ~ we honor our symbiotic relationship. We discover ways the plant world lives within our bodies and souls.

Let's begin our exploration of Water and Plants, as we did last chapter, with a story. Although this story, *The Water of Life*, was told by my Sufi teacher,[8] its theme is universal and is told in many other traditions, as well. After listening, we will *Breathe in communion with Water*.

THE WATER OF LIFE

Once, in a faraway land…or was it right here, where we are today?…there lived a young shepherd. His life was simple and he was content among the hills, singing or playing his wooden flute as he kept watch over the flock.

Now, he knew the land in which he lived as well as if it were his own skin. He knew the rhythms of the day and seasons of the year as well as he knew his own breath. It was in this way that he knew the moods of the weather and the perfect time each morning to open the gate as his sheep flowed into the day. He knew where in spring the early greens would appear first. He knew the places with deepest shade and brought the flock there when the sun shone hot and bright. He knew the folded hills and where to find the richest grasses. He knew to take the flock to the high meadows in the hot months; while grasses scorched below, they were still fresh among the hollows. Each day, regardless of the season, he brought the flock to drink and rest beside a narrow brook at the foot of the mountain. They escaped the heat while listening to the song of the water and the wind among the branches. The brook brightened and ran more quickly, to hear the voices of the sheep and the shepherd's music approach. In the autumn the shepherd harvested fodder to keep the sheep through the winter months. Each spring he sheared the flock and brought his wool to market.

At market, his wool was the first to be bought and always brought the highest price. People marveled at the high quality, and word spread to arrive at market early, to procure his best. This cycle persisted for many years. He cared well for his sheep, they drank the sweet water and rested each day beside the streamlet; the wool from his sheep was the best in the land.

As years passed, people noticed that not only were this simple man's sheep fat and healthy, but he himself seemed to never age. When asked, he simply smiled and said, "We live among the hills. We drink the pure water." Soon people came to him asking for a cup of this magical water for an ill child, or a pitcher-full to bless a wedding. The small brook joyfully gave her gifts away, and everyone this water touched flourished with well-being.

A small village sprang up not far from the hillside brook. The people lived in happiness and brought gifts of gratitude to offer the pure water for its blessings. People floated flowers downstream, some balanced favorite stones by the water's edge. Children splashed in the clear shallows; they grew strong and kind. The water of life was plentiful and joyfully gave of her blessings!

Word of these waters of life eventually reached the king's ears. Quickly he sent messengers to verify these accounts. Upon their return he gathered a great party of courtiers and soldiers and set out to see this wonder. At their arrival, the villagers ~ surprised but honored ~ hurried to guide the king to the hillside stream. Children played, the sheep bleated in the cool shade of trees, the shepherd played his wooden pipe.

Seeing this idyllic tableau, the king wanted this goodness for himself. A great silken tent was erected nearby, and he sent for the queen. He proclaimed, "As this water flows in the midst of my kingly lands, I claim all rights." A summer palace was built. He gathered his greatest thinkers to plumb the depth of this mysterious water. A high fence was built around the springhead and pool; guards stood nearby night and day. The royal doctors set about examining the properties of the healing waters, and soon a university sprang up. Students from many lands paid highly to come and study the water. Philosophers debated the meaning of the waters, while artists came to paint and sell their canvases at a high price. Chefs set up eateries and entertainers sang and danced upon a stage. People traveled from far and wide, waited for hours ~ sometimes days ~ to pay for a single sip.

But without the shepherd and his sheep, without the children's laughter and the flower offerings, the water of life was lonely. The high fence kept her old friends away. Now she was accompanied only by the guards who rolled dice in the shade, or those who poked and prodded her banks, who took her waters without a glance of gratitude. Now she bubbled and sang hurrying down the hillside no more. Her waters ran slow, flat and murky. The doctors, the professors, the philosophers…no one noticed that though this water still flowed, it no longer held life within its appearance.

Crowded out of their village, bothered by the dust and noise, the shepherd, his flock, and the poor villagers had packed their few belongings and walked away, to find a new home. A long while later, they saw a green hill with trees fruiting and birds calling. Here they planned to stay the night, before moving on. As they ate their journey-bread and settled among the bundles for sleep, the shepherd took out his wooden pipe and began to play a sweet haunting melody. Suddenly, a bright gurgling sound was heard; a crystalline stream of water poured from between two nearby boulders. It sparkled and sang as it tumbled down the hillside. People, sheep, children and the water of life all rejoiced again in each other's company. The people settled down in this place, living their simple lives, close beside the banks of the once-again shimmering generous waters.

Breathe in communion with Water.
Now let's sit, holding the images of this story as we breathe in unison with the grace of Water. Let us greet Water with honor and gratitude:

Beloved Sister Water, I greet you with Gratitude and Love.
  Your holy waters travel the waterways of my being.
  Your flow inspires my life voyage.
  Your purification washes me clean.
  I am dissolved in your ocean of love.
I give you honor and praise.

- Sit comfortably and relax, breathing in through the nose and out through the mouth, as though blowing through a straw.

- Enjoy a few breaths and relax into the rhythm.
- Imagine you are standing in a quiet rain, or in a small gentle waterfall.
- Be aware of the water touching your skin, softly sliding down your body.
- Be aware that you are an integral part of this flowing stream of water.
- Notice that the water not only moves smoothly over your skin, but also moves through the interior of your body.
- Feel the sparkling water swirl through all your liquid systems. Be aware of the water pushing downstream any stagnation in your backwaters.
- Become one with this liquid grace.
- Relax into the continuous flow of grace; breath by breath be revivified.
- Continue flowing with this sacred water, for Water is Life.
- End with a deep bow of gratitude.

Water in the Outer Landscape ~ Water as a Gift from the Stars

Water Is Life

There are many ways Earth exists in the "Goldilocks zone," for everything we need is in the habitable sweet spot. In the vastness of the cosmos, our position is unique. We are not too close and not too far from our star; we are "just right." This is particularly true of water; if we were a bit closer, our planet would be scorching like Venus, and water would evaporate immediately. A bit further away from the sun, like Neptune, and water would be deeply frozen ice. This position makes our water *just right* for life to evolve. We are the only planet in our solar system to have accessible water.

This accessibility of water on Earth occurs as stable bodies of liquid water on the surface: streams, tributaries, rivers, lakes, wetlands, deltas and oceans. We have deep deposits of water underground, in aquifers that are continually replenished by rainfall. We also have deposits of ancient waters ~ fossil water ~ formed in the original shaping of the Earth. Water graces us in solid forms as well, in our glaciers and ice caps; also in atmospheric ice and water vapor, as well as in the magic of snowfall.

Earth and our bodies are both composed of approximately seventy percent water. 97 percent of this water is saline and contained in oceans, while only 3 percent exists as fresh water. This is a clarion call to protect our hydrologic cycle, which provides us with the rare and precious gift of fresh water!

Our water, like the minerals that formed earth, came as *gifts from the stars*: it came from comets and asteroids. As these celestial bodies collided with Earth, much of their water was transferred to earth, where it was able to remain ~ neither burned away in the atmosphere, nor frozen as ice. Some have posed the Theia hypothesis: there is a possibility that a twin planet collided with a newly-forming Earth. This collision may have given Earth a larger core as well as doubling Earth's water. It may also have created our Moon. When I think of this, I am reminded of the eternal love relationship between the Moon and the oceans; the waters always following their original love. Some scientists postulate that three billion years ago, earth was entirely a water world.

THE MIRACLE OF THE WATER CYCLE

The hydrologic cycle is taught in grade school: water from lakes, rivers, and oceans evaporates, enters the atmosphere where it cools, condenses into liquid water, and comes back to Earth as rain. But science now has a much more detailed picture of this multidimensional miracle of collaboration between the water element and the plant realm.[9]

Ocean water evaporation is driven by the energy of the sun. The sun heats up the air and ocean surface, causing water molecules to evaporate. In the atmosphere these molecules cool and condense into liquid. But what is it that causes this liquid water to not simply drop back into the ocean? Why does rain travel inland?

As earth cultures have always known, and science is finally discovering, *trees and plants call the rain.* Trees release small organic particles called aerosols; these allow water vapor in the air to condense around them, bringing rainfall to these forested areas. All vegetation helps to increase rainfall, but it is important to know that in forests, the size of the tree is important. The older, larger mother trees can draw water inland many more miles than younger ones. Trees that grow along the banks of rivers create atmospheric corridors that bring rainfall deep into continental interiors. By this we can clearly see how deforestation breaks this life-giving natural cycle.

An amazing component of the water cycle that is newly being explored is the role that fungi play: mushrooms are rainmakers. These earth-bound beings have been classified in the plant realm for many years. Recently, though, scientists have learned that fungi are more closely related to animals yet are a unique and separate life form. They are now placed in their own realm, the Funga Realm. We are beginning to more fully understand the relationship between flora, fauna and funga. An individual mushroom can release thirty thousand spores every second, with a daily output of billions of microscopic particles. "The dispersal of vast numbers of these spores into the atmosphere above forests has a significant role in the condensation of water in clouds and the formation of raindrops."[10] Again, we see that deforestation breaks the ancient collaboration between water and plants, as well as water and funga.

Urbanization, with its centuries-long practice of deforestation, also breaks the water cycle. In forests and grasslands the vegetation exudes the natural particulates around which water molecules coalesce. These organic particulates are right-sized to create rain. It is in this way forests call to oceanic waters. Amazingly, forests also create their own rain clouds due to water condensation on the underside of leaves. Cities and industrial areas also create atmospheric particulates ~ pollution ~ but these industrial aerosols are too small to constellate condensation and bring liquid rain. The heavy gray skies, smog and humidity are a result of this damaged rain cycle.

All plant life supports the water cycle by not only calling the rain, but also slowing water absorption into the soil. In a forest rain falls through the foliate umbrella from leaf to leaf, slowly entering the soft loam below, which is light and friable from autumn's annual mulching process. Prairies operate in a similar manner, as green plants slow rain's entry into the nutrient-rich porous soils created by the decomposition of yearly stubble. This slow water absorption feeds streams, tributaries, rivers, and recharges underground aquifers. Full streams and rivers further support plant and animal life; this we call a virtuous cycle.

WOUNDS AND REPARATIONS

Human mismanagement of the living water cycle, as well as our squandering of this precious gift, endangers all life. Deforestation brings desertification and salinization, while mechanized irrigation depletes aquifers. These destroy water's virtuous cycles and usher in the vicious cycles we see world-wide: drought, wildfire, flood, famine, disease, war, refugee crises, and more.

Yet we humans are also implementing healing solutions, many of which have been practiced by native peoples for millennia. Earthen water catchment ponds are transforming drought-stricken lands;[11] agro-forestry, native to ancient Africa, is increasing; indigenous fire-management systems, employed worldwide in the past, are being reintroduced; new and traditional regenerative farming practices are blooming; the restoration of beavers to arid landscapes is proliferating in America's West; worldwide tree-planting projects focusing on native trees are being implemented by local people.[12] All of these promising ways are bringing healing and restoration.

How do we in our individual lives become part of the solution? Here are a number of ideas, many of which are already familiar: Become involved in your local watershed protections. Turn the shower off to soap up and shampoo, then on again to rinse. Make the loads larger and do less laundry. Put a sign above your toilet "If it's yellow, let it mellow. If it's brown, flush it down." Buy water-saving appliances: washing machines, dishwashers, toilets. Plant native gardens. Make your lawn into a vegetable garden. Make water gardens which are beautiful water catchment systems.

Of equal and perhaps more importance, we must deepen our personal relationship to the Element of Water; we are naturally compelled to protect that which we love! Love is the only answer powerful enough to turn the tide. Let's turn our attention now to Water in the Inner Landscape.

Water in the Inner Landscape: Alchemy and the Transformation of Self

The Water Element in the inner landscape mirrors water in the exterior.

As in the exterior landscape, in the inner landscape Water's positive qualities are life-affirming: the ability to flow, to accept grace and intuition, to have ease with relationship, the capacity for accommodation, for cleansing, rejuvenation, and buoyancy; also the ability to purify and dissolve the old as preparation for the new.

Worldwide water rituals portray these qualities. Throughout Christianity baptism is practiced soon after birth or after an affirmation of faith. The baptismal waters that accompany the birth of life in the spirit mirror the amniotic waters that birth us into the life of the physical world. It is noteworthy that some of these practices entail complete immersion in an actual river or pond. Five times a day Muslims worldwide practice the ritual water purification called Wudu as a preparation for prayer, for merging with the holy of holies. Within Judaism Mikvah is a ritual of washing in preparation for prayers and holy days. Hindus bathe in the holy waters of Mother Ganges to wash away karma and prepare for death. Jesus washed the feet of his disciples as a model for service to the world. These water rituals offer us powerful images of washing away the old and making way for new beginnings.

Water in the interior can also carry challenging qualities; these challenges arise when our inner water is out of balance. Notice how many common figures of speech use water images. Out-of-balance water can show up as indecision, a tendency to be wishy-washy. Mood swings can arise when we are tossed by the waves of emotion. Sometimes the waters of life come toward us like a river running fast; without an inner rudder we can feel easily overwhelmed. When our inner boundaries are not firm, we can feel that we are drowning in ours or other people's emotions. Some people have a tendency toward the melancholic, toward seeing the cup as half-empty.

DISSOLUTION AS THE WOMB FOR NEW LIFE. Sometimes life asks or demands of us a particularly difficult aspect of water: *Dissolution*. We have all experienced this in large and small life events. Perhaps we have made exciting plans for a new project and find at the last moment they are washed away by unforeseen circumstances; they dissolve, and now we are lost ~ where do we go? Or, much harder, we may find a pivotal relationship is ended, and not by our own wishes. We are dissolved in sorrow and not sure who or how to be, as we move forward. Dissolution *will* come calling on us. How do we learn to be in relationship when dissolution is required?

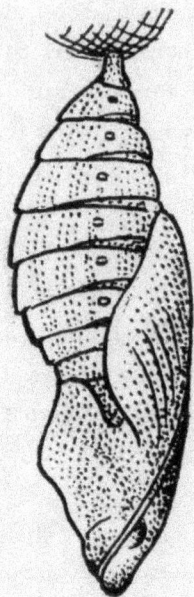

Chrysalis of Apatura clyton.

Images[13] are the way our heart understands emotion and therefore learns how to feel. Story images can help us navigate when big emotions arrive unbidden. At these times it is helpful to imagine and meditate on the life of the butterfly. We sit quietly and feel our way into the experience of the caterpillar who spins herself into a silken nest, a cocoon. There the chrysalis slowly and entirely *dissolves* into a primordial goo. Allow the sensation of dissolution: everything familiar is deconstructed and regenerated into raw potential. Feel yourself falling into slow time, for the cycles of nature ~ and human nature ~ unfold in exquisitely slow detail. To everything there is a season: it is when the season has warmed and ripened enough, when all is prepared for new life, this is when the cocoon opens. We emerge entirely transformed. This total dissolution has been necessary for the next stage of our evolution. As John O'Donohue reminds us in his poem "For the Interim Time":

"What is being transfigured here is your mind,
And it is difficult and slow to become new.
The more faithfully you can endure here,
The more refined your heart will become
For your arrival in the new dawn."[14]

Think, as well, of sugar that must let go of its crystalline form and become liquid sweetness to flavor our morning tea. Powdered yeast must dissolve in warm water to become a fragrant loaf of bread. When dissolution arrives, it is essential that we bow to this life event; that we lay down our long-prepared plans, allow enough time for complete transfiguration to dismantle the old and for new growth to emerge from fresh ground. Letting go is foundational to transformation. When we learn to let go and allow transformation to move and shift us in the many small ways life asks, the process can become filled with grace. These small and large life events provide us practice at letting go, in preparation for the eventual letting go that we all will encounter at life's end.

How do we learn to let go? Slow down. *Breathe*. With each exhalation feel your heart soften. Melt and allow dissolution to become more permeable with each breath. Feel the breath swinging through your heart. Your own heart is the safe, nurturing place for transformation to be incubated. Allow yourself to be rocked and cradled by this healing breath. With this comes rest, rejuvenation, and time for the New.

INQUIRY QUESTIONS FOR THE INNER LANDSCAPE:

a.   Do I have inner seeds, soul dreams, that want to be watered? Is my soul calling me, but I am timid, afraid? Do I make myself too busy to listen? Do I have a deep inner wish, but choose inaction and resentment? How do I water this soul dream? What does it need in order to blossom?

b.   Is there "drought" in an aspect of my life? Do I live in my head? Am I isolated, or defended? Is my work-life deadening? How can I call rain (grace) to come?

c.   Is there a knot in myself that needs softening? Am I clutching an old wound? An old self-image? Am I holding an old anger? How do I slow down; allow grace to fall and soften like rain?

d.   Am I water-logged, boundary-less and suffering because of it? Am I moody, overwhelmed with emotion? What will balance this sogginess?

Plants in the Biosphere
The World Tree

Water is the mother of all life on Earth and her earliest life form, aquatic plants, arose around 700 million years ago as algae. Ancient algae's vast palette of green and red hues helped catch the light needed for photosynthesis, while water offered support to the algae helping them to catch as much sunlight as possible. Plants migrated to land about 450 million years ago and became the womb of life on land. Plants' production of oxygen altered the atmosphere and this in turn allowed for the evolution of animal life.

If you are interested in exploring more of the science about plant evolution, you must read Elisabet Sahtouris' *Earth Dance: Living Systems in Evolution*. There you will find her beautiful description of chloroplasts and mitochondria, ancient organisms that she calls "bubblers and breathers." Her description of the primordial ways these beings evolved from competition to collaboration is an important lesson for humanity. Humans contain this map that leads from aggression to cooperation written into our most vegetal ancestral memory. When plants first arose, it was a very short time before they had populated Earth in a variety of ways, from grasslands and scrub to vast regions of primeval forests.

Plants create the air we and all animal life needs; we breathe in symbiosis with these arboreal relatives of ours! They are a crucial element of the water cycle, as we learned above, in that they call the rains which recharge the aquifers as well as regulate the absorption of moisture into soils. They drive weather systems and provide wind breaks on land, while mangroves protect coastlines by reducing the height and energy of wind and waves passing through them. Trees provide shade which modulates temperatures and helps soils retain moisture.

While a few of us in western cultures may be familiar with plants as medicine, 80 percent of people worldwide rely on them for some aspect of primary healthcare.[15] It is not only land plants that offer medicine, ocean kelps also promote health in myriad ways, and plant medicine is even airborne. As we walk among the trees, especially in an old-growth forest, we are immersed in an air bath of natural forest medicines released as a fine aerosol mist. Tree aerosols have anti-cancer properties, improve circulation and decrease high blood pressure.[16] Plants touch every aspect of our lives in countless ways. They provide us with food, building materials, clothing, shade, comfort, beauty. Plants have a profound effect upon the stability of our mental and emotional health.[17]

In any discussion of plants, it is crucial to include the plant realm's intertwined coevolution with land, insects, birds, animals and humans. Landforms, plants, animals and humans would not exist in the form they now inhabit without our millennia-long love relationships together. The plants' reproductive system is the ancient antecedent to our own. Our brains, veins, arteries and nervous systems carry plants' aboriginal shapes. We are bound to the plant realm physically, emotionally, mentally, and spiritually. Their well-being is our well-being.

Given this symbiosis, as plant communities become more endangered by deforestation, mono-cultures, GMOs, pesticides and habitat loss, we help to heal these wounds and be good relatives in a variety of ways. We can give loving attention to house plants, or grow a small organic garden. Perhaps we learn about and employ biodynamic agricultural principles, or support Community Supported Agricultural farms that work on these principles. We research and get to know our farmers, as well as proactively source where and how our other groceries are produced. We use herbal medicines or even know our herbalist. Let's support local native plant endeavors and make compost for pollinator gardens.

How to Consciously Make Relationship with Plants in the

Inner Spheres

Let's return to our practice of visualization, as we did with Minerals. Let us greet the Plant Beings:

Beloved Plant Beings,
Your branches are reiterated in my veins.
You are my food, medicine, clothing, shelter.
Your shade brings cool midday relief.
You are my elders and teachers.
We breathe in the symbiosis that is love.
I give you gratitude and love.

VISUALIZE OUR PLANT-SELF:

- Let us again settle into our body. Allow our awareness to drift down from the head and rest more deeply in the region of the heart.
- Allow the breath to swing through the heart; you may feel that you are a child again, swinging in your back yard, from a long swing on the branch of a tree. Or perhaps you have an ancient memory of being rocked in a cradle.
- Be aware, in this movement, of how your breath enters and exits your being as pure gift. You need make no effort; life-giving breath simply arrives with fresh energy and buoys you up, lifting and filling not simply your lungs, but your whole being with the *new*. New oxygen is created fresh for you, the sublime gift given by our Plant relatives.
- Be aware that this gift of breath also carries away the old ~ old energy, old thoughts, old patterns ~ whatever we are ready to let go. This is given back and recycled, by the benevolence of the trees' roots and their mycelial allies.
- Allow yourself to slip inside the skin, the bark, the trunk; slip into the consciousness of your favorite tree.
- Become aware of your tree-self in your womb/reproductive region, pulsing warm and vibrant, about three fingers

below your navel. We inherited the seeding, growing, fruiting, cycling, dying, and resurrecting qualities from our plant ancestors.

–   Trees are the keystone species on planet earth. We humans can join Plant Beings as a sister-keystone species, enriching and supporting all life.

–   Be aware of bare winter trees, whose intricate, eloquent limbs are reiterated in our branching veins and arteries.

–   Be aware of your brain as a neural tree.

–   We breathe in symbiosis with trees; let us do this consciously:
    *On the inhalation, breathe minerals up from your roots and cosmic light down through your limbs.
    *On the exhalation feel your blessings being sent as "aerosols" into the world. These blessings are medicines as surely as the trees' exudates.

–   Be aware of life-giving water flowing up through your being: we and the plant realm are the living marriage of heaven and earth. Water is the connecting principle.

–   Stay with this symmetry as long as you like. When you are ready, return to your human form. Bow and give thanks.

Questions to Deepen Your Relationship with the Plant Realm

Choose a tree or plant to be with on a daily basis for a week, or longer. To follow a plant through the round of seasons is an education all its own! Be with this plant relative at different times of day, to become aware of its response to different weather, light, moisture ~ to learn its moods, its likes and dislikes. Notice the other beings that come to partake of its generosity. Offer gratitude and honor each day as you:

–   breathe in unison with your Plant Being

–   with respect ask these questions:
    What does it *feel like* to be you?
    What gifts do you bring me now?
    What do you need from me in turn?

End with several breaths. *Offer Blessing to Water and Plants.* Commit to explore your relationship with Plants more fully as you move through your days.

DEEPENING PRACTICES FOR CHAPTER TWO

Again, for this chapter, we will bring our learning into all aspects of our being: into our bodies, hearts and souls, as well as our minds. We will inform our bodies with action: giving care and attention to our Place for Honoring the Realms, and our Gratitude Bundles. We will educate our heart and soul by collecting images and feelings and will give loving imagination to our Kinship Collage. We will enrich our life of thought by mindfully attending to our internal inquiry questions and recording them in the Journal. All of these offer gratitude and blessings to Water and Plants.

PLACE FOR HONORING THE REALMS: OUTDOOR SIT-SPOT OR INDOOR NATURE SPACE

Now we bring Water and Plants to join our Earth and Minerals. You might go out to cut some spring greens or flowers for your altar, transplant an herb into a small pot, or bury a seed in your bowl of Earth. Place a bowl of water within your honoring space to help bring flow and livingness. Each day greet the Plants and change the Water. Give honor and thanks for the qualities of purification, revivification, accommodation, and flow. Bow and smile.

CREATE A GRATITUDE BUNDLE FOR THE WATER ELEMENT AND REALM OF PLANTS

Our Earth is composed of 70 percent water, and we ourselves are composed of as much as 60-70 percent water as well. Water is the Mother of Life and all Earth cultures have honored water for her gifts of balance, revivification, harmony, purification, and flow. Water flows through our bodies and the bodies of our more-than-human cousins, especially the Nation of Trees. Trees are integral partners in Earth's hydrologic cycle; we can emulate the trees and become intermediaries in the water cycle too.

We take the blessing of water into our bodies, psyches, and souls and then return the gift of purity, fluidity, and balance to all life. It is our gift and responsibility to honor and express gratitude to Mother Water; we do this by offering "Earth Prayers," our gratitude bundles. In this way, we nourish the Element of Water and the Realm of Plants.

- As you did last chapter, you can begin with either a piece of paper or a large leaf. If you choose paper, paint or color an image that represents the Water Element and Realm of Plants, or write a poem to honor them.
- Now you gather the items you'd like to offer. Fold in the manner we discussed before, in a way that honors earth, sky, generosity and encircling protection. Tie the bundle as before.
- To give away this gratitude bundle, go to water. Here, you send your bundle downstream. If you prefer, you can tie the string onto a root to secure the package; let the prayers float downstream till finally it disintegrates. If it is a pond, you can float it and watch it sink, as you generously give it away.

Create your own prayer, or use the following as a springboard. Make your prayer audible ~ sing or speak ~ as you give the offering:

Beloved Mother Water, you are the generous giver-of-life. You sustain all life on Earth with your joyous rainfall, cold and clear mountain freshets, your tributaries; they congregate to become broad nourishing rivers. All waters, including the water that flows as Gift through our bodies, long to return to the saline life-producing waters of the Oceans. We give you honor, gratitude, and love. Please accept this prayer bundle from my deep heart.

KINSHIP COLLAGE

Choose images that represent the *Water Element and Realm of Plants*. Create a collage that integrates these Water Beings into the unified whole that we experience here on our watery and green Earth!

REWILDING HUMAN NATURE JOURNAL

Record your work with the Questions for Inner Inquiry into your relationship with Water, as well as practices to deepen your kinship with Plants.

CHAPTER THREE

The Fire Element and Animal Realm

Tending the Sacred Fire ~ Animal Spirits

I N THIS CHAPTER we explore our relationship with the Fire Element, embracing fire's qualities of purification, warmth, enthusiasm, creativity, and especially transformation. Here, we learn ways to create an inner "hearth" and "container," in order to work in dynamic relationship with fire, mindful that we not be consumed by its brilliance. Let's also explore ancient systems within the living Earth, which continue to be practiced today, that create outer containers for the intensity and creativity of fire. We will live into the ways fire transforms the landscape, as well as the landscape of the soul.

We also step into the intelligence and agency of the Animal Realm, discovering how our furred, feathered and finned cousins live directly inside our brains and bodies. We explore ways to live more closely into our own "soft animal bodies," and thereby become sensitively aware of our interdependence ~ our Interbeing ~ with our vast family of animal cousins.

Let's begin, as before, in the traditional way and hear a story. This tale tells of the deep connections humans have with animals, including the intimacy of shape-shifting. First, though, a few thoughts about these ancient relationships:

Many earth-cultures, ancient and modern, believe that "the Animal People have spirits that enter the human world and give their bodies to supply humans with food, fur and other materials. After their flesh is used the animals return home, put on new flesh and re-enter the human world again, whenever they choose."[18] The aliveness of this relationship principle can be seen particularly in the preparations for the hunt. Hunters learn to "slip inside the skin" of their prey through ceremonial dance, in which they become one with the spirit-animal. Through these sacred ceremonies and stories, the people are educated and informed in respectful ways of being human. For instance, one is taught during the hunt to wait for the individual animal who will "give himself." This story of the far north Yupik people shows us a glimpse into the generous mind-set: the unity between the human being and the food we eat. This story is often told around the fire during evening celebrations of a successful seal hunt. After hearing this story, let us *Breathe in communion with Fire.*

A YUPIK TALE OF THE HUNT

We are told the Seal People have kind feelings about human beings; they recognize us as their younger siblings and know, therefore, that we need help and guidance through life. Because of the Seal People's good-heartedness, a young hunter once went to live and learn with them.

Soon he found himself underwater, dressed in a seal-skin garment. His host seal-family showed him the various ways of seal life. From them he also learned the way seals perceive human beings, how they help and teach humanity. One day the seal colony saw hunting boats paddling out into the ice and, because they love to watch our human ways, they hurried along to swim close-by. The seals told the boy that if he wanted, he could choose a boat and its hunters. He could "give himself" as a gift.

Their instructions were concise and clear: if he saw a boat that was unkempt, dirty and not well-repaired, he should understand that this is the boat of lazy, selfish people; they do not honor their boat by caring for it. As such, they also would not honor his gift or share his flesh with the village; instead, they would hoard it. These were not the sort of people likely to help the women and children or to respect and honor the old people. On the other hand, if he saw a boat that was well-tended, bright and beautiful, if he saw the respectful countenances of the hunters, and heard their songs of the hunt, he would then know that these were the best sort of humans, worthy of his gift. They would offer a wonderful celebration for the entire village, full of music, song and dance. They would sing of his generosity and their thankfulness. They would honor him and the generosity of the sea.

One thing we may not know is that the Seal People are mesmerized by human voices and drumming. They are swept away by human singing, dance, and the beauty of the feast. The seals told him that if he chose to give himself, when the spear pierced his flesh, he would slip out of his seal-skin garment. His spirit could then climb into the boat and return to the village with the humans, to join the festive preparations. At the moment before dawn, he could choose to slip back into the sea and be given a new seal-garment, or he could stay among the people to be born soon as a human baby.

The boy-seal did as he was told; he chose a wonderful hunting boat and began to swim close beside it. He surfaced again and again, looking to catch the eye of one of the hunters. Soon a shining young man exchanged glances with him, the spear entered his seal-flesh, which he gladly gave to the hunters. As his spirit sailed back to the village with the hunters, he relished the hunter's songs praising his generosity to the entire village. That evening at the feast he strolled among the people. Their faces glowed with gratitude. Their laughter, song and dance, children's games...the fire...everything delighted him.

At the moment before dawn he hesitated...would he return to live among the humans again? But no, he chose to slip back into the sea, his new seal garment awaiting him.[19]

Breathe in communion with Fire.

Now let's sit and hold the images of this story, as we breathe in unison with the power of Fire. Let us greet Fire with honor and gratitude:

Beloved Father Fire, I greet you with Gratitude and Love.
    You are the generative force.
    Your fire illumines the Universe; your light makes love visible.
    You awaken seeds in the dark and kindle ideas in my mind.
    Your power of transformation gives rise to all life.
I give you honor and praise.

- Sit comfortably and relax, breathing in through the mouth with lips slightly pursed, and out through the nose.
- Enjoy a few breaths and relax into the rhythm; feel the warmth.
- On the inhalation be aware that this breath acts as a bellows and sends a direct and penetrating airstream into the center of your solar plexus.
- Feel the divine spark being blown upon and flames beginning to leap up.

- On the exhalation be aware of the growth of this flame of life.
- Continue to feel the fire warm and radiate through your heart, your body, and soul.
- Allow the warmth and radiance to penetrate through your skin, vitalizing and invigorating all that is around you.
- Slowly become aware that this fire produces not only warmth, but light.
- Continue to breathe fire into the solar plexus and feel light ray out through your heart.
- Allow this warmth to radiate and the light to illuminate your whole being as well as those around you. Become the life-giving sun! Let your light touch the stars.
- End with a deep bow of gratitude.

Fire in the Outer Landscape ~ Fire as a Gift from the Stars
Tending the Sacred Fire

Earth-wisdom cultures offer us stories of gifts that have come to Earth from the stars. Fire is one of these essential bequests. In African lore among the Kuba people, Mbombo, the creator god, was also called Bumba. Bumba created all the lands and creatures including Tsetse, the lightening, who lived in the sky. Eventually humans began to complain to Bumba, as we often do. Now they wanted something new ~ to eat food that was cooked. Bumba solved this problem by instructing Tsetse to send her lightening from the skies into the African trees. Bumba then showed the humans how to harvest this fire for their hearths.

Native American Cherokee stories also tell of a time when there was no fire on earth. Only Thunder's companion Lightning had fire. Thunder saw the animals and people were cold and hungry, so asked Lightning to carry fire down and place it in the great hollow trunk of a sycamore tree. The story goes on to tell how the animals, who must swim across a lake to the burning tree, took turns till they finally managed to bring a branch with still-glowing fire back across the water.

It is evident in the stories science currently offers, as well, that fire has come to us from the stars. It is this star-fire that powers our own star the

Sun and that sits in the belly of the Earth; the mitochondrial fire in each of our cells is born from the stars, as well. Again here, we find that Earth exists in the "Goldilocks zone." Earth is the only planet in our solar system that has "free" fire: fire that is available to burn. Other planets do not have Earth's abundance of oxygen, which is necessary for combustion. We thank our tree-relatives for their gift of oxygen.

The Greek myth of Prometheus echoes this theme of gifts coming from the stars, with a uniquely western twist. Rather than working with the principle of "The Gift" Prometheus steals fire from the gods. They, understandably, are angry and he is given eternal punishment. He is not punished because the gods wanted to keep fire from humanity, rather, because he stole it. He did not wait for it to be given as a gift, neither did he give proper gratitude and honor. It was his hubris that brought about his punishment. Perhaps this theft of fire, and its consequences, continues to live with us: we no longer remember fire with respect and gratitude.

David Abram, visionary geophilosopher, offers this window into the deep respect given to the Goddess of Fire. "Across the Pacific, among the Ainu people of northern Japan…the household fire was herself a goddess who could see all that unfolded around her; she would report back to the other gods whether the animals taken by the hunt had been treated with proper respect."[20] In the twenty-first century, though, we are willing to break this relational bond with fire that humanity has always honored.

We no longer look to the natural world to learn when and where fire is to be used. Indigenous seasonal burns, which were practiced for millennia, were informed by this close observation. We squander fire as we guzzle electricity for entertainment and escapism. Think of the billionaires whose "Space Race" is a thinly disguised plan to escape a ruined earth. How much rocket fuel (fire) did it take to put a billionaire in space for four minutes? It took 5.5 billion dollars. Six billion dollars could have saved 47 million people from dying of starvation. We trade human lives and brazenly squander fire for our own pleasure.

We no longer "touch" fire. Fire is banished from our daily lives: from cooking, from producing light and heat, from sacred ceremony. We forget to ask as well as to give gratitude. How often do we remember to be grateful when we turn the thermostat up?

We have broken this sacred relationship and continue in Prometheus' footsteps. We steal fire every day; we are even willing to break open atoms to steal the fire inside. Is the climate crisis a natural consequence? Having been banished from the realm of the sacred and reduced to the convenience of "climate controlled" homes, it may be that Fire is finally declaring "If you will not acknowledge me in my sacred form, you will see me in my wrathful form." Perhaps there are other than strictly environmental reasons for the current proliferation of wildfires.

RELATIONSHIP IS THE ORIGINAL CONTAINER OF FIRE

Is there a way that we can weave together the relational synthesis of earth-wisdom cultures with the observational analysis of western science? Can we bring these seeming opposites into an integrated whole? Annette Lee, a Lakota and Ojibwe artist and astrophysicist, is one of a growing number of indigenous scientists who advocate for "two-eyed" seeing: the braiding together of Traditional Ecological Knowledge with western science. She founded Native Skywatchers[21] to preserve knowledge and educate others about Indigenous star stories. Her site is a gorgeous coming-together of science, culture and art. Robin Wall Kimmerer is a very visible model of this seeing with two eyes, as well.

Original cultures have always practiced two-eyed seeing. They do not separate spirit from nature, nor separate keen ecological observations from deep reverence for the spirit that permeates matter. Humans have had deep relationship with fire for millennia. Neanderthals, who lived for three hundred thousand years in harmony with earth, used fire as they sculpted the landscape to encourage its productivity. Earth cultures continued this practice, using fire to steward forests, grasslands, steppes, water ecosystems and care for all the attendant animals that these enriched environments supported. *It is the power of respectful relationship that is the container of fire.* Lyla June Johnston[22] sees humanity as having been a keystone species, using fire and other methods of traditional ecological knowledge to expand and design many different ecosystems for the benefit of all life. She affirms that not only can humans restore our relationships and return to our original keystone position, but that we *must* do this!

What does reestablishing relationship with fire look like, in the twenty-first century? Here is one example. If you heat your home with a wood stove, you know how important it is to know the "moods" of the stove, the qualities of the wood, to know how the wind affects the draw. You learn the size and shape of the coal bed at different times of day, the size and type of wood for various situations. Fire becomes a friend that you know very well, anticipating its ins and outs, the needs of the moment and what the next few hours will bring. In this way you become a participant in the dance between yourself, the fire and your wood stove.

Respectful relationship with fire is also being reestablished in the Western United States. California and Oregon are partnering with local native tribes to learn the ancient practice of "good fire on the ground." The Karuk, Yurok and Miwok peoples, among others, are working to reintroduce seasonal prescribed burns in forests and grasslands, and the Yosemite National Park fire managers are on board as well.

In our daily lives with our children, or when we gather with friends and family, we too can move more closely toward fire. We can make a fire pit in the back yard, build a small fire and tell stories as the moon rises and fireflies dance. We can bring a flute or guitar and sing as owls hoot in the treetops. We can roast hot dogs and marshmallows on a snowy afternoon. If we live in an urban area, we can still bring the living flame into our life. With electric lights extinguished, candles at dinner bring alive the magic of fire. A long soak in a hot bath by candlelight will influence our dreams and visions. When we approach fire as a sacred gift we mend the rip in the world. Our ancient ancestral memories that flow through the blood and in our DNA are reignited. We become whole again in communion with sacred fire.

Fire in the Inner Landscape: Alchemy and the Transformation of Self

The Fire Element in the inner landscape mirrors fire in the exterior.

Fire operates in similar ways in both the outer and inner landscapes. Fire is life-affirming; it is heart-warming; enthusiasm is the child of fire, born from fire's spark of inspiration; like the sun, fire is charismatic ~

all flowers turn toward the solar warmth and light; fire is energetic and dynamic; it is passionate and spontaneous; fire is also an agent of transformation, burning away the old to make fertile ground for the *new*.[23]

We can be aware of the gifts of positive fire in our lives in many ways. Like the sun that shines generously on all life, our own generosity is fire's gift. The warmth of our interest in others mirrors the sun's warmth which penetrates into the earth's soil, and into the shallow coastal waters, promoting life's proliferation. Our warm interest penetrates others' souls and gives nourishment. Fire's gifts are so numerous! Fire lives in us when we are courageous and undertake an expansive project; when we step with steadiness into an unknown situation; when we speak up for ourselves or others; when we can face adversity without over-reaction.   Fire's spark of inspiration comes alive and must be followed as enthusiasm, for the idea fuels us with vigor and energy. "Fire seeks to transmute everything into light, into its higher nature! It is the transforming power of fire that allows us to evolve and become illuminated."[24]

When fire is in an unbalanced state, though, it offers us challenges. Think of the challenge of wildfire in the forest. We must not only address the immediate danger and work toward fire's containment, but after the conflagration, it is imperative that we examine the causal circumstances. We must look into past fire management practices and reassess these, in order to make the land more fire resilient. In the inner landscape, as well, we address the current flaming emotions, explore the causal elements and alter our actions for the well-being of the future. Fire's imbalances can look like frustration, anger, burning desire, impulsiveness, abuse of power and more. As with wildfire, when addressing imbalanced inner fire we need to repair the immediate damages, discover the causes and take steps toward remediation.

Our balanced relationship with inner fire opens doors to its positive energy and power in our life. Without cultivating this relationship of awareness, we remain unconscious. We can tend to either ignore the lessons fire offers, or on the other hand to become overwhelmed by its quick intensity. With conscious cultivation, we can find the right ways for fire's intensity to be healing and transformative.

Meditation on an image can be helpful, as we discovered in the last chapter's image of the caterpillar's transformation to a butterfly. A powerful alchemical image that portrays humanity's intimate relationship with fire is the alchemical image known as The Salamander in Fire. The salamander, held in dynamic equipoise amidst the flames, affirms visually that it is possible to *Hold the Balance* come what may.

HOLD THE BALANCE AMIDST THE FLAMES
It is crucial in the inner landscape that we *not deny*, push down, or refuse fire as it comes into our life. To deny the fire of frustration or impatience is similar to the US Forestry Department's one hundred years of fire suppression policies. We need to engage the frustration, find out what is at the root, discover if there are exterior or interior actions or attitudes that need to change and proceed forward. To suppress inner fire's challenging aspects can spill over into denial of fire's positive qualities of warmth, enthusiasm, creativity and transformation.

It is also imperative that we *not feed* fire's challenging aspects. When anger arises, we need not rant either outwardly or inwardly, not indulge in fantasy arguments. Rather we take the anger inside and hold it, examine it, tend it. Question it: where did this begin; follow the root back. Did my words or actions spark an unintended insult? Is this a pattern in my life? Can I speak or take action that will be a remedy? Like tending a campfire, we poke it with a stick. We stay with the flames and watch them become coals, burning low, becoming productive.

How do we remain steady, like the salamander in the flames, when *strong* fiery emotions arrive unbidden? How do we respond when we can find no word or deed that will help? Earth and water are elements that help to contain fire. Let us turn toward earth. Take a long walk and feel the rhythm of your footsteps and breath, as they hold the fire; run and feel the fiery power of your legs pounding the trail; work hard ~ rake a mountain of leaves or scrub the basement floor; chop firewood and feel the deeply satisfying thud of the axe biting the wood. Let fire burn through you with vigorous activities. In this way we metabolize the fire, without burning others.

Water also controls fire. Our brain can't process happiness and anger at same time, so think of what brings you gladness and delight. Singing? Take a walk and sing loud! Put on your favorite music and dance! Do you play a musical instrument that you adore? Do you just love working out at the gym? Or a long slow yoga session? What brings *you* upliftment? When you engage in happy activities, there is no room left for the anger.

Let's look at the function of the woodstove. Its purpose is to provide an appealing, accommodating place where fire can live in equanimity at the center of your everyday life. We can make our own physiology ~ our body ~ become a container that gives the inner fire a balanced place in our life. We do this, again, by looking toward earth and water as balances. Earth practices are rhythmic: Go to bed at the same time each night and sleep enough. Rest during the day ~ take short breaks. Eat healthy meals at the same times. Exercise enough daily. Spend plenty of time in nature. Water practices bring happiness: Make time to share your heart with friends and family. Engage in a hobby that brings you joy. Water is movement, so be sure your life is filled with enough satisfying physical movement. Feed your senses with luscious beauty ~ nature, art, human nature.

The *creative fire* is a double-edged sword and it is good to know how to make relationship with this trickster; it can so easily shape-shift from bringing enormous positive energy to bringing us down with a crash. Think of how many of our society's creative artists, musicians, or activists flame up bright in youth, but are burned to a cinder by midlife. They turn to drugs and alcohol to tamp down the flames, or they even die young. Creativity is fire indeed, and I'm sure we are all familiar with the astonishing burst of light that accompanies a new inspiration. We are literally on fire with enthusiasm; this a good and necessary surge to accompany the "launch" stage. But we must learn to temper the fire ~ to be equal partners with fire and be sure that our fundamental bodily, social, and emotional needs are met. Let us not become "moths to the flame," consumed by the creative fire. Let's remember that even the creative fire is contained by earth and water activities.

What do we do when life gives us a conflagration? This Holy Fire, the fire of transformation, arrives when an inferno is necessary: *some seeds open only by fire!* As with other aspects of fire we have discussed, we can make relationship with this in similar ways. We do not deny it, nor feed it. We rely on earth and water practices to balance and help contain it. The Salamander in the Fire becomes our guide; we survive the flames and look for green new shoots of life.

Perhaps some of us need to cultivate more fire.
What about those who would like to encourage fire as a balance to an overly watery or earthy inner life? Perhaps we swim about in the waters of emotion feeling deeply but lack inspiration and purpose. Or maybe we go about our dailiness with a lock-step determination but feel life is too routine? Here are a number of ways to introduce the enthusiasm and transformation of fire.

*Practice the fire breath in the morning, feeling on the inhalation life's bellows blowing on our inner spark. On the exhalation, become aware of the flames leaping up as warmth and light pouring forth into the day. Throughout the day, take a breath of fire and feel its spark enliven you.
*Bring the living flame into your life on a regular basis. Perhaps

weekly or seasonally, with consciousness and intention, kindle a sacred fire in the back yard. Sit by this fire, gaze into it, give it your attention, listen to its wisdom. Make a fire offering to the Spirit of Fire.

*Once a week prepare a nourishing meal for your family, light candles with a song, and enjoy the firelight flicker as you eat.

INQUIRY QUESTIONS FOR THE INNER LANDSCAPE

a. What lights my fire? What sparks my enthusiasm? Is there a good healthy dose of this in my life? If not, how do I court enthusiasm?

b. Where do joy and vigor appear in my life? At home? In my work? In nature?

c. Do I need courage in order to move forward; do I need to face something I've been avoiding? What is the first step toward courage? What is the next step?

d. Is the fire of transformation ~ the Holy Fire ~ bringing a challenge to me? If so, how do I respond: how do I hold the center? Can I look for the shoots of new life?

e. Is something burning as a wildfire in my life? How will I contain it? Earth? Water? Both?

We carry this star-fire within our bodies, psyches and souls. But we humans were not the first living beings to carry inward fire. As mammalia-morphs, our ancient ancestors, suddenly transformed from being cold- to warm-blooded, new behaviors, habitats and ways of living became available to them.[25] The fire of the stars and the fire in the belly of the earth is the same force that catalyzed this movement from reliance on outward warmth to inner mitochondrial combustion. We share this inner warmth with our animal cousins. Let's study the role they have played, and continue to play, in making our life on earth filled with beauty.

Animals in the Biosphere

Animals, plants and landscapes have coevolved together. Animals' grazing and foraging patterns shape and powerfully impact a region's vegetative growth. They also distribute throughout the landscapes of their migratory routes seeds caught in their fur. They distribute, as well, nutrients present in their scat. In this way animals are "ecosystem engineers," they shape vegetative terrain, landscapes and water-scapes.

For instance, we know that ancient elephants helped to create African ecosystems, and they continue to function in this way. During the dry season, they use their tusks to dig up dry riverbeds and create watering holes many animals can drink from. Their dung is full of seeds, making good habitat for dung beetles, as well as helping plants spread across the environment. In the forest, their grazing on trees and shrubs creates pathways for smaller animals to move through. In the savanna, they uproot trees and eat saplings; this keeps the landscape open for zebras and other plains animals to thrive.

Beavers engineer landscapes by building dams across small streams. This dam building transforms rivers into complex wetland systems that support a diversity of water and land species. Beaver activities increase biodiversity, reduce soil erosion and retain sediments which improves water quality through increased filtration. Beavers create wetlands which store water during drought, as well as minimize flood risk.

When native animals are separated from the landscapes they coevolved with, these landscapes suffer in myriad ways. Wolves were recently re-introduced to Yellowstone Park because in the one hundred years of their absence from the park, the entire ecosystem had fallen out of balance. Coyotes ran rampant, and the elk population exploded, overgrazing willows and aspens. Without these trees, songbirds began to decline, beavers could no longer build their dams, so riverbanks started to erode. With the reintroduction of these top predators the ecosystem is returning to balance.

Earth wisdom traditions have always seen animals as elders and teachers. Science is catching up with this ancient wisdom: some evolutionary biologists theorize that wolves were early human's first teachers.[26] Humans may have observed wolves, who were their fellow predators, and learned useful strategies for the hunt. Early human-wolf collaborative hunting practices were common, and wolves may have begun domesticating themselves to early humans as early as one hundred thirty-five thousand years ago. Because wolf pack behavior and human family behaviors are similar, it became an easy next step for them to view each other as fellow family/pack members. Things have not changed much: think of all the family portraits that include the beloved family dog! We may be able to quantify the many benefits of this early wolf-human alliance, but we can never measure the love, friendship and compassion both species enjoy together today.

Perhaps it was our cousins the wolves that taught us one of our most human characteristics; did they teach us how to play? Humans continue to have playful relationships not only with our domesticated family animals, but with other animals as well. Amazonian communities play "tag" in their canoes with river dolphins, for no reason other than fun. The dolphins come up beside fishermen in their boats and tap them, then dash away. The fishermen hurry after and tap the dolphins with their oars. This game can go on and on. Island people as well as many others love to swim out and play with a pod of porpoises. Ravens and crows love to play and have been friendly with humans for eons. Inuit legends describe how Crow brought light to the far north for his people, and the Norse god Odin was informed about the goings-on in the world by his two ravens.

Animals also develop "working relationships" with humans. Fishermen in Myanmar call dolphins by tapping sticks in rhythm along the sides of their canoes to mimic the sounds dolphins themselves make. The dolphins cooperate by herding fish into the fishermen's waiting nets. Without the nets to push prey into, the dolphins would not be able to catch fish as efficiently; conversely the dolphin's help significantly increases the success of fishermen. They cooperatively share the catch. Sometimes dolphins will wake fishermen that fall asleep in their boats, encouraging them to keep fishing. In Africa, humans and the honey-guide bird work together in collecting wild honey. If the birds see a bee-tree that has begun to split, they will come call the villagers to help. The villagers bring their machetes and open the tree further. The humans take their share of honey and leave the rest to their colleagues, the birds and honey bees. The villagers also sometimes go into the bush and mimic the honey-guide's call, inviting them to accompany the honey gathering adventure. There are many other current animal-human alliances. They also remain alive in countless worldwide fairy tales of friendship and partnership, like the Seal Hunt story and more.

Ancient animals live inside our human brains. Here is a quick tour of how our animal cousins inhabit our bodies. Our brain developed from the olfactory bulb (the smeller) of two-hundred-million-year-old tiny mammals. Our lungs began as gills. Paul McLean, the twentieth century pioneer of brain science, coined the term "the triune brain." Our brain stem and sensory/motor brain were bequeathed to us by the reptiles. Our limbic relational brain is a gift of early mammals. Our right hemisphere, whose domain is holistic thinking and synthesis, comes from our primate elders. Our left hemisphere, whose domain is thinking by analysis and taking things apart, evolved with ancient humans. Our prefrontal cortex, the CEO of our multi-species brain, is what McLean and colleagues called "the angel lobes." Here we find humanity's finest qualities: altruism, empathy, selflessness, and more.

Animals share our outer landscapes, as well as live inside our brains, bodies and especially our hearts. How can we cherish, honor and protect them? Here are a few ideas:

*Move more toward a plant-based diet.

*If you do eat meat, be sure ethical practices are used as it is raised.

*A simple act of love is to put up bird feeders; then study how to correctly provide food and water. Don't forget shrubs and greenery will offer protection from predators.

*Support organizations that protect and care for animals

How to Consciously Make Relationship with Animals in the Inner Spheres
Spirit Animals

Let's return to our practice of visualization, as we did with Minerals and Plants. Let us greet our Animal Cousins:

Beloved Animal Cousins,

You are humanity's elders.
Your voices educate my heart.
Your wisdom informs my mind.
Your warm presence comforts my animal self.
Your friendship brings me health and joy.
I give you Gratitude and Love.

VISUALIZE OUR ANIMAL-SELF

- Let us again settle into our body. Allow our awareness to drift down from the head and settle more deeply into the region of the heart.
- Allow the breath to swing through the heart; you may feel that you are a child again, swinging in your back yard, from a long swing on the branch of a tree. Or perhaps you have an ancient memory of being rocked in a cradle.
- Be aware, in this movement, of how your breath enters and exits your being as pure gift. You need make no effort; life-giving breath simply arrives with fresh energy and buoys you up, lifting and filling not simply your lungs, but your whole being with the new.
- Turn your attention now to your solar plexus, just below the sternum; feel the breath moving in and out of this powerful center.
- Feel your solar plexus as a radiant source of warmth and light.
- Allow your attention to move with this radiance out beyond your skin, into the world.
- Feel these solar rays touching the world.
- Now begin to look around with the eye of your heart: where do you find yourself?
- At the top of a mountain? In the shallow waters of a coral reef? Are you in a primeval forest? A desert? In your back yard? At the city park?
- When you have settled into your landscape, noticed its features and flora. Now become aware of animal presences sharing this place with you.

- What kind of animals are with you? Herd animals on a prairie? Wolves at the periphery? Electrical eel among coral and kelp? Eagles in their eyrie? Great blue heron at water's edge? Black bear eating berries? Backyard squirrels and chipmunks?
- Now notice that one of these animals is watching you, interested in you.
- Return this interest. Breathe a few breaths together. Enjoy their presence.
- Make eye contact. Look into the face of a completely different reality.
- When you feel ready, ask our Internal Inquiry Questions:
  *What does it *feel like* to be you? Through empathy, understand and share their feelings.
  *Why have you come; what gifts do you bring to me?
  *What do you need from me, what can I give you?

End with several breaths. *Offer Blessing to Fire and Animals.* Commit to explore your relationship with Animals more fully as you move through your days. Do you have a spirit animal, or perhaps the animal you met in the above meditation, who feels like kin? Greet this animal cousin each day. As you walk, keep them at your side; look at the world through their eyes. Move the way they move, "speak" with their voice.

DEEPENING PRACTICES FOR CHAPTER THREE

Again, we will bring our learning into all aspects of our being: into our bodies, hearts and souls, as well as our minds. We will inform our bodies with action: giving care and attention to our Place for Honoring the Realms, and our Gratitude Bundles. We will educate our heart and soul by collecting images and feelings and will give loving imagination to our Kinship Collage We will enrich our life of thought by mindfully attending to our internal inquiry questions recording them in the Journal. All of these offer gratitude and blessings to Fire and Animals.

PLACE FOR HONORING THE REALMS: OUTDOOR SIT-SPOT OR INDOOR NATURE SPACE

This chapter, we will bring Fire and Animals to join our earth, minerals, water, and plants. Bring a central candle or place four candles at the corners of your sacred place. Do you have seashells or small animal bones you have found on woods-walks? Perhaps small, finely carved wooden animals? Add these to your altar with gratitude and respect.

Each day, light the candle(s) and greet the fire. Bow to all the mineral and Plant Beings. Welcome especially the Animal Beings. Give honor and thanks for fire's qualities of purification, warmth, enthusiasm, and creativity. Bow and smile.

CREATE A GRATITUDE BUNDLE FOR THE FIRE ELEMENT AND REALM OF ANIMALS

The perfectly balanced Fire at the core of our Earth is the warmth that fosters and enfolds all life. Without this balance, our planet would be either a giant icy rock hurtling through cold space or be consumed by an inferno. This cosmic fire that inhabits Earth is the same fire that illumines the stars, as well as the mitochondrial fire that combusts in each cell of all animal bodies, including our own. We recognize the gift of balanced fire, as it warms our earth and all our bodies, hearts, and souls.

It is a human privilege and responsibility to give honor and gratitude to the life-giving warmth of Fire; we do this by offering "Earth Prayers," our gratitude bundles. Let us nourish the Element of Fire and the Realm of Animals.

- Again you can begin with either a piece of paper or a large leaf. If you choose paper, paint or color an image that represents the Fire Element and Realm of Animals, or write a poem to honor them.
- Now you gather the items you'd like to offer. Fold your bundle as before, in a way that honors earth, sky, generosity and encircling protection. Tie as before.
- To honor fire, go to the living flame; either an outdoor

fire or a simple candle indoors. To offer your prayer bundle you can burn it in an outdoor fire and bring the ashes (your purified intentions) to nourish the garden. Or, you can make a very simple but sacred bundle on a single sheet of paper. Hold it by tweezers over the candle flame. Again, you give it away. In this way, you nourish the Element of Fire and the Realm of Animals.

Create your own prayer, or use the following as a springboard. Make your prayer audible ~ sing or speak ~ as you give the offering.

Beloved Father Sun, ancient peoples have known you to be the sacred preserver of life. Your balanced warmth calls sleeping seeds to rise up into your light, wakens animals from long cold winters and inspires us to emulate your generosity in our own hearts. It is your Fire that combusts inside each of our cells, bringing life-giving energy to us and our Animal cousins. We ask that we learn to carry your balanced Fire, that we learn to draw down the human-induced fever the earth now suffers from. We strive to find this balance in our own lives. We give you honor, gratitude, and love. Please accept this prayer bundle from my deep heart.

KINSHIP COLLAGE

For this chapter choose images that represent the *Fire Element and Realm of Animals*. Create a collage that integrates these Fire and Animal Beings into the warm and unified whole we experience as the Universe.

REWILDING HUMAN NATURE JOURNAL

Now you'll record your work with the Questions for Inner Inquiry into your relationship with Fire, as well as practices to deepen your kinship with Animals.

CHAPTER FOUR

The Air Element and Human Realm

Gaia's Breath ~ We Shape the World

IN THIS CHAPTER we breathe into the Air Element, discovering vast spaciousness within our being and experiencing the "breath of Gaia" that moves through us. This breath connects us in living relationship with all beings. We breathe the same air created for us by ancient trees: all breathing beings share this equally. As we breathe with all beings, we will remember what the Organization of Nature Evolutionaries' Pam Montgomery says: "We are breathing ancient sunlight!"[27]

We are aware that it is air that allows us the capacity for human speech; it is the medium through which other beings, as well, vocalize and communicate. We discover ways to listen to the wisdom that is carried on the wind, as our Earth Ancestors speak to us. We breathe in symbiosis with all our plant mothers and our four-legged cousins.

In these pages we will also look into the complex and often divergent capacities of the human being. What ideals do we carry? Who models these qualities for us? Can we breathe in communion with the breath of our teachers? We will learn ways of using the breath as a navigational tool through life's travels.

Let's begin, again, in the traditional way. Let's hear a story about the deep connection we have to the Element of Air. We long for the freedom of air. Lacking wings with which to catch the wind and fly, we learned to weave sails that allow us to fly across the waters. After hearing this Japanese folk tale, we will *Breathe in communion with Air.*

THE CRANE MAIDEN

Once upon a time in faraway Japan there lived an old man and his wife. They were very poor, for the old man had been a simple sailmaker all his long life.

Though they owned very little, their modest needs were met. All but one need, that is; the old couple had always wished for a child. Now, especially in their old age, they longed for a child's companionship. In the evenings they sat on the porch of their small hut, atop a breezy hill, looking into the green marsh below. Here they consoled their loneliness with the sight of the graceful white cranes that came to nest and raise their young in the warm shallow waters of the marsh. In flight, their wings and strong, fine feathers reminded the old man of the way his sails caught the wind. It pleased him to think of himself as a weaver of wings.

One dark and stormy autumn night the old ones sat indoors, close beside the warm fireplace. Amidst the wind and beating rain they heard a hard thump upon the door. Opening the door, the old man saw a crane lying upon the porch; it had been blown there by the furious winds. The old man brought it indoors where he and his wife warmed and tended it, giving it water and food. To their delight, the crane remained with them for a few days until it became strong. On the third morning after breakfast, the crane opened its majestic wings and with a backward glance of thanks, it flew silently into the fine blue-sky wind. As the old woman saw its grace and beauty, the feathered wings reminded her of living sails.

Winter came and went. The old people were delighted to welcome the spring green as it crept back into to the marsh and to marvel as the returning cranes glowed white amid the grasses.

One day as the old man sat on the porch weaving at his loom, he saw a small figure climbing their hillside path. As it drew closer, he saw this was a young woman. But she walked so slowly and bent, as though carrying a heavy burden. When she came close he called to her, "Come and let us give you tea." The young woman arrived and sat down, exhausted. When the old wife brought tea and they sat to drink together, she noticed the young woman's wrists were thin and her cheeks hollow. Slowly the old people began to ask the girl about her life, but all she would say is "My name is Tsuru-san." She stayed with them for the afternoon and that evening they shared their simple dinner with her. Afterward she quickly fell asleep, so they covered her and went to bed themselves.

In the morning they discovered that Tsuru-san had wakened early, started a small fire in the stove and was now cooking rice and preparing tea. They were happily surprised, but dared not hope that she would stay a while longer. Day by day they expected her to continue on her way, yet she remained with them helping with chores and fetching water from the well. It was not many days before she began to sing in her quiet voice, color returned to her cheeks and often there was a sparkle in her eyes. The old couple realized she must have been orphaned; but now could Tsuru-san become the daughter they had so often longed for?

Springtime came and rolled slowly into the deep green of summer. The old people's daughter remained with them, helping with the many tasks their weakening eyes and hands found difficult. All three were happy and the hut was often filled with laughter, song and good food. But with the chill of autumn the old man's arthritic hands could no longer separate the threads upon the loom. Struggle though he may, the threads were tangled and no completed sails were made.

One day Tsuru-san came to her parents and said, "I will weave a sail for you, and thereby care for you in your old age." They were so surprised! They had not only the gift of a daughter, but a sailmaker as well! Yet Tsuru-san asked one promise, "You must not watch me as I weave." Surprised, the old man said, "But I also am a sailmaker, why can I not watch?" Tsuru-san said only "You must promise!" And so they did.

Tsuru-san pulled a curtain between them and began to work. The old ones could hear the shuttle sliding and the loom rocking. This gentle song filled their hearts. The day passed and night arrived. Tsuru-san continued to weave as the loom rocked and sang. Husband and wife slept. At dawn when they awoke, they continued to hear the loom. Late in the morning when Tsuru-san finally finished, she looked tired and spent. They worried about this, but when she placed the sail in their arms they forgot everything but the magnificent sail.

Although it was immensely strong, the sail weighed nothing at all! The old woman heard a whispering and put her ear to the folds of the sail. Her eyes became wide: Tsuru-san had woven the wind into the fabric! The old man walked to the harbor with the magic sail and was paid enough gold to live for half a year. Overjoyed, he returned home to his wife and daughter.

Time passed. The family was happy that winter and wanted for nothing. In spring, though, the gold was gone. Once again, Tsuru-san offered to weave a sail. This time she repeated her instructions "You must not watch me as I work. This will be the last sail I can weave for you; it takes so much out of me! Promise you will not watch me, now!" The old parents agreed and Tsuru-san slipped behind the curtain.

A full day passed and all they heard was the song of the loom as it rocked against the floor. This time it took two full days and when Tsuru-san emerged exhausted, she held a sail even more beautiful than the first. It, too, held the wind. *Thinking of the gold, not of his daughter's exhaustion, the old man went to the village and sold the magic sail. This time there was enough gold to last for nearly a year. They were overjoyed, yet the old mother worried for her beautiful daughter.*

It was not long after this that a great trading ship arrived in the harbor. The fame of the magic sails, woven of the winds, had traveled far and the ship's captain came in search of the weaver. Asking among the people, everyone pointed him toward the small hut at the top of the hill.

Arriving there, he said to the old man, "You must weave a magic sail for my ship! I will give you gold enough that you will never need to weave again. Weave for me one sail and you will enjoy a life of ease!" The little family all gasped! Never weave again? They would have all their needs met for the rest of their days. But Tsuru-san hesitated, "The sails take so much of me...they take my very life." Her mother agreed and said, "No Tsuru-san, you have given us so much already." Tsuru-san saw, though, the disappointment in her old father's eyes. She bowed her head and said, "I will weave this one last sail for you. But promise me you will never look!" She pulled the curtain and began.

One day passed and then another. The song of the loom filled the air, yet even on the third day Tsuru-san had not finished. The old parents looked at each other; what could be wrong? Worry, and curiosity as well, drove them to the curtain. They pulled it aside. But it was not their beautiful daughter who looked up at them with her shining eyes. No, it was the crane the old man had saved in the storm. She was weaving her own feathers into the sail on the loom. "Tsuru-san!" they cried. Filled with sea wind, the feathers were trembling.

Their crane daughter could give no answer, but her eyes were full of sadness. Then she spread her tattered wings, lifting herself through the window and into the sky. Filled with grief, they watched her graceful flight as the wind carried her away. She flew further and further away from the old people and their life together, disappearing into the feathered clouds.

Never again did the old people see Tsuru-san. With the gold from the final magic sail, they lived their last years in ease. But each year in the autumn season of storms, they waited, hoping to hear a knock upon their door.[28]

Breathe in communion with Air.
Now let's sit and hold the images of this story, as we breathe in unison with the freedom of Air. Let us greet Air with honor and gratitude:

Beloved Brother Wind, I greet you with Gratitude and Love.
   Your wind is my breath.
   Your breeze is music in the treetops.
   The leaves and my soul dance to your melody.
   You bring me the blessings of all beings.
   Together we breathe the One Breath.
I give you honor and praise.

- Sit comfortably. Relax, breathe in and out through the mouth with lips slightly open.
- Enjoy a few breaths and relax into the rhythm.
- On the inhalation become aware of air wafting into your whole being, swirling through your limbs and organs, spiraling around your spine, expanding to fill your whole self.
- On the exhalation be aware of air ~ your breath ~ moving out and beyond your skin.
- Breathe a few breaths with this expanded awareness, more fully with each breath.
- On the inhalation imagine the green beings who have created this air for you.
- On the exhalation send gratitude out toward your plant relatives. Take a few more breaths enjoying our symbiosis.
- Become aware of all your animal kin who have breathed this air before you; let the wind in their wings become your wings, let the breeze ruffling their fur become yours, feel the whales' breaching of the waves, as water sparkles off your own back.
- Become aware of a river of feathered, furred and finned relatives' breath flowing into your being, and moving out as well, carrying your blessings along with theirs.
- Now be aware of your human ancestors; breathe several breaths with them.
- Now be aware of your human beloveds who are present with you; breathe with them.
- Now be aware of your descendants who carry you into the future; breathe with them.

- Become aware of the gift and blessings offered you in this way. Breathe gratitude.
- Allow your blessing of love and gratitude to mingle with theirs, moving out and blessings the world.
- Hold the Earth and all her earthling children within the protective circle of your breath.
- End with a deep bow of gratitude.

Air in the Outer Landscape

Gaia's Breath

When we looked at Earth, Water and Fire, we began our exploration by recognizing that they come to us as gifts from the Stars, from the Cosmos. Yet breathable air, which contains adequate free oxygen, comes to us as a gift from the Plant Realm. Minerals, Water and Fire arrived from cosmic processes. But with the plants a new magic arose, a home-grown magic. Earth Magic.

A few other planets have evidence of small amounts of oxygen, but this is tied up in mineral and liquid processes. Only Earth has "free oxygen." This is similar to the way that Earth alone has "free" fire. Again, we gladly find ourselves in the Goldilocks zone. Earth's oxygen supply originated with cyanobacteria, tiny ocean-dwelling organisms that survive by photosynthesis. Oceans continue to produce 70 percent of the oxygen on earth. The majority of this production is from oceanic plankton ~ drifting plants, algae, and some bacteria that can photosynthesize ~ which creates oxygen. It is earth's high percentage of oxygen, 21 percent, that has allowed for more complex life forms to evolve.

Air is the unifier: every breath we take has been created by the Plant Realm for us. The air we breathe this very minute has been breathed by hundreds of thousands, millions other beings ~ furred, finned, feathered, scaled, as well as other humans. *Take a breath now. On the inhalation be aware of the imprint of countless fellow beings. Follow this breath on your exhalation as it moves outward, to fill the lungs of endless others. Imagine every aspect of yourself as a great lung…all of yourself filling with this tender elixir composed of all our relatives' breaths. Take a few more conscious* breaths. Now consider your exhalation: what qualities of being do you want to breathe into this potent brew?

Air is also the comforter, the healer, the guardian: Let's think about it this way. When water passes through its stream and riverbeds, the minerals it encounters influence the structure of the water. Viktor Schauberger,[29] the early twentieth century Water Wizard, says at the springhead water is innocent, like a baby. But as it journeys to the ocean, it has experiences with minerals which help it to be shaped and to mature. We can taste these experiences that water has as it interacts with minerals. Like different wines, different waters have very different characteristics.

Within Sufism it is said humans have a similar opportunity, with the air we breathe. As air moves through us, we can consciously choose how we want to influence the air we pass on to others. We "imprint" it with blessing, protection, healing, abundance, generosity etc. Many others of our ancient ancestors understood their relationship and responsibility to air in the same way.

Earth wisdom peoples commonly felt that our thoughts are carried on the wind, and they considered the air itself as the embodiment of Spirit. In Arabic and Hebrew, the word *Ruh* means spirit, breath and wind. Air also carries our thoughts into the world as spoken word. Remember Genesis begins "In the beginning was the Word. The word was with God and the word was God. And the word was made flesh." Here we see air as spirit, and as spirit made manifest as well. In most oral cultures, *the word* was considered sacred; *the word* was the manifesting force. In world tales we find the power of speech is essential. Often the hero or heroine is told "You must speak your desire." It is understood that speech brings desires to earth; speech helps to shape the future.[30]

Sound is a formative force. Sound waves are carried on the air and impact outer reality. I learned this as a young woman when I visited the Exploratorium, a science museum in San Francisco. In one of the exhibits, sand was sprinkled onto a metal plate. Classical music was played and wired to the metal plate. The sand began to dance in response to the sound waves affecting the plate. It formed itself into flower shapes and mandala patterns, following the changing sound patterns! If physical substance (sand) is shaped by sound waves carried on the air, imagine how we ~ infinitely more malleable than metal ~ also are shaped by what we hear and speak. Noise pollution adversely affects the lives of millions of people. Studies have shown that there are direct links between noise and health. Problems related to noise include stress-related illnesses, high blood pressure, speech interference, hearing loss, sleep disruption, and lost productivity.[31] We have the gift of choice, though. We can choose what we listen to; we can craft our soundscape to a large degree. We can choose the words we send out upon the air as well.

What we think, breathe and speak has huge impact in the world; it creates the present and informs the future. Joy Harjo, US poet laureate, tells us "Remember the wind, her voice. She knows the origin of the Universe." Think of the many voices calling from all quarters; declaring it is time for humanity to change the story, to change the way we think and speak life on earth. Let us be like the water, that absorbs and passes minerals along her journey. Like the air that picks up the scent and the medicinal essences exuded by plants. Let the air move through us, pick up our generous and healing thoughts, and carry them to the ends of the earth. Let our healing spoken words reverberate in the dome of heaven.

Here is a thought-question for us to consider: how deeply are our thoughts and feelings carried on the airwaves, influenced by the multilayered environment in which we find ourselves? Let me share an experience that I find to be consistent; I wonder if you experience this as palpably as I do? When I am indoors, in the built environment created by and for humans ~ with all the attendant human-related sounds, air currents, electrical humming and buzzing ~ I find that my thoughts and intentions, my feelings and questions are filled with human concerns. But when I am walking in the forest, sitting beside the sea with salt breeze in my hair, or at a favorite woodland water pool ~ as I listen to a distant fox's bark, the cry of gulls or the buzz of dragonflies above the water ~ my thoughts are suddenly free, my understanding is multidimensional, my feelings are wide and expansive! The constraint of walls dissipates. The living languages spoken all about me enter my whole being as I breathe; these more-than-human thoughts circulate through my bloodstream, side by side with the oxygen. How does this work for you? Notice this as you contemplate this chapter: how do your thoughts and feelings differ when in nature and when indoors? How do the stable, right-angle walls affect your thoughts and feelings as compared to the fluid, round, slightly-in-motion thoughts that come to you beside a creek or when leaned against a tree?

Air in the Inner Landscape: Alchemy and the Transformation of Self

The Air Element in the inner landscape mirrors Air in the exterior.

In the image above[32] we see a medieval alchemical depiction of the Spirit of Air. As we contemplate this figure we feel the all-pervading power of Air. Air operates in similar ways in the inner landscape as well as the outer. Let's look at some of the qualities of Inner Air. Looking into a clear blue sky we see the qualities of clarity, openness, spaciousness, equanimity, freedom and transcendence. We experience these air qualities in our inner life when we slow down our pace, settle into a steady rhythmic breath, move out of our head and into our body. We transcend the racket in our monkey-minds and attend to deep sensory immersion in the current moment: the rustle of leaves in a breeze, the song of summer evening's crickets, our children's laughter from the bathtub.

When we attend to air in our inner lives we find the realm of the inner Witness, as well. We have a sense of the overview; from here we can discern patterns both interior and exterior. Discovering patterns helps us to make meaning of life. Inner air offers us both curiosity ~ wondering how things work ~ as well as the capacity to create life-imbued concepts. Inner air can also bring us toward the realm of Spirit. Within some branches of Tibetan Buddhism the breath (air) is called The Wind Horse, a name for Spirit. As mentioned above, in the Arabic language the word Ruh connotes *breath as Spirit*.

Inner air, when in an imbalanced state, can create challenges as well. Without enough water and earth ~ without enough rich loam and moving water ~ we can become cool, aloof, and haughty. We can see our self as above the nitty-gritty of life. This self-inflation results in an inability to connect with life with all its vulnerabilities as well as its glory. We can become all thought and no action. Becoming all mind, we lack guts and elbow grease ~ we lose the capacity to manifest our ideas. We cannot bring them down and *earth* them. We become lost, building castles in the clouds, spinning daydreams. Without the ground and liveliness of earth and water, we can become drawn toward dogmatic ideologies, as well.

There are many ways to invite the Air Element into dialogue with our inner landscape. When we feel too much pressure, too many demands, too much intensity in our lives, we can elicit the spaciousness of air. This is the way I invite air's spaciousness: On the inhalation, I call upon the wide blue sky, opening out to the expanse of the cosmos. I am aware of earth's deep ocean of air, of its generosity as it flows into my being, blowing through all my cells. On the exhalation, I feel my hard skull become less dense. It becomes a vapor and mingles with clouds moving through blue sky. My mind is filled with breeze and birdsong. A few breaths of this spaciousness reset my balance. I have more space with which to address life's concerns.

When something unexpected and unwanted occurs, we need the balanced non-reaction that air offers. We can invite air in this way: Now we move the breath through our heart. Feel the breath swing into the heart center on the inhalation and feel it swing back out on the exhalation. Be aware of this swinging, this rocking. Perhaps you remember this from childhood. Be rocked and cared for by this subtle movement of the breath through your warm heart. Allow your heart-breath to expand enough to *make room* for this unexpected and unwanted event. Stay aware of the breath rocking you, caring for you, while facing the challenge.

When life gives us a riddle, offers a conundrum that leaves us perplexed, call on air to bring the overview. When we attune to air we can step back from the personal perspective and see the whole picture. Taking this long view, breathing slowly and looking through life events, we begin to see our patterns. We see how they fit together to compose the whole. We begin to see purpose and thereby discover meaning. We harvest nourishment from the life we live.

How do we find meaning within the patterns of our life? With the movement of the breath gently rocking us, we ask these questions: "Where did this pattern begin? Whose voice is speaking?" We notice "Oh…here I am in this situation again." In this way we catch glimpses of the pattern. Staying with the breath, we compassionately ask ourselves "Where is the root, what is the underlying need that creates this repetition?" Staying with the compassionate breath and the healing movement, as breath rocks us, we *feel* the need. We ask our wise heart and expansive breath, "How can I have what I need in a more positive way? How can I change my attitude or behavior?" When we learn to step back, untangle the threads and understand more deeply our own personal life events, this overview can help us to witness large world events with more equanimity and compassion.

We practice and deepen relationship with Air in simple powerful ways. Although simple ways are always *simple*, they are often not easy! Throughout the day, in quiet moments, be aware of your breath. Be aware of the trees who have created this air for you. Be aware of all the beings whose bodies this breath has passed through before you. Be aware of all the beings who will be breathing this breath, which contains your imprint and blessing, in the future. When you are outdoors and a breeze arises, greet it with honor and love. Allow it to carry all the cares of the day away; send love out on this gentle breeze, toward a world hungry for compassion.

INQUIRY QUESTIONS FOR THE INNER LANDSCAPE

a. Is there a situation in my life that is asking me to take the overview?

b. Do I feel cramped in an arena of life and need to breathe spaciousness into it?

c. Where can breath help me be non-reactive?

d. In looking for meaning, what wisdom does my heart-breath offer?

e. What new ideas, projects, seeds are being breathed into me now?

f. Is there anything in my life that is "pie in the sky," "airy-fairy?" How will I "earth it," ground it, bring it down to manifestation?

Humans in the Biosphere

"In a gentle way we can shake the world." Ghandi

In the last chapter we discussed the limbic/relational brain gifted to us by our mammal ancestors. Humans are also bestowed with a unique thinking capacity and, as we know, "thought is carried on the wind."[33] As we study humanity, a good place to begin is to become familiar with the prefrontal cortex (PFC). The PFC is evolutionarily the newest part of all earthlings' brain structures, and the human PFC is three times the size of other primates.[34] Located in the center of the forehead, the PFC is directly behind the "third eye," which is recognized by many Eastern traditions as the seat of humanity's highest consciousness. In fact, Paul McLean, known as the finest twentieth-century pioneer of brain research, and his colleagues called this area the "Angel Lobes." It is the domain of executive function: the CEO of brain function. Among its many duties, it has the dual aspects of the organizer (the linear planner) and also the caregiver (the holistic nurturer.) The PFC chooses how to use the capacities of the evolutionarily earlier brain structures ~ the sensory-motor and limbic relational structures ~ for specifically human needs. What this means is that the PFC chooses how we engage with the gifts of the senses (how we perceive) with movement (what we do) and with relationship (how we love.) The most important piece we need to remember about the PFC is this: *it is environment- and experience-dependent.* This means the lessons we learned in childhood about what it means to be human, as modeled by our elders and society, these become neural pathways and are hard-wired in our mind, psyches and actions. And yet, the brain remains malleable forever; we can consciously choose to lay down new neural pathways, new ways of being human.

In humanity's infancy matriarchal cultures, also called "linking" societies, predominated. Matriarchies generally follow the principles of the earth herself. These principles involve cooperation, collaboration, decentralized power (many beings' brains are decentralized and distributed throughout the entire body) egalitarian decision-making (think of starling murmurations), and generosity. The care and well-being of women, children, land and waters were the foundation of all decisions.[35] Women are the life-bearers. Children are the future. Land and waters are our sustenance. Plants and animals are our relatives and allies. So, if the PFC learns how to operate ~ how to be human ~ by the thoughts, feelings and actions modeled by our elders and the society at large, this means early matriarchal societies imprinted humans' angel lobes with these qualities of care-giving and generosity. Most societies consider these to be our finest.

Yet, due to climate catastrophes and waves of invasions, patriarchal ~ or ranking ~ societies overran these cultures of peace and prosperity. The starkly different ways of being human, built upon principles of domination and exploitation, became imprinted into humanity's prefrontal cortex. Most modern societies live with the following principles:

*competition and therefore
*domination in all sectors of life
*ranking people according to merit ~ not need
*males hold authority over women, children, and property
*property is viewed as "resources," not gifts to be stewarded
*individual ownership has shattered the wealth of the commons
*common goods such as healthy earth, clean water and air have become monetized
*extraction, exploitation and domination reign

In spite of patriarchy's spread throughout societies, there has always been a quiet thread of consciousness that points toward the matriarchal values of care, generosity, cooperation and equality for all.[36] I have always loved the Sufi view that we are born with all the necessary equipment to become Human (with capital H, meaning our finest self) but it is our upbringing, our training, and our spiritual path that shape whether we turn toward egoism or altruism. This agrees with what science shows us about the PFC: we become the sort of human that we see modeled before us. But because of the malleability of the brain and the gifts of the prefrontal cortex, *we can choose.* In adolescence or adulthood, our heart and soul can prompt us to seek out models that align more clearly with our own personal values. We then apprentice ourselves to these models and begin the journey, as the Sufis say, toward becoming a True Human Being.

Who are the people in your life that model the sort of human you want to become? Whose "subtle atmosphere" do you want to slip inside?

*Family members?

*Ancestors?

*Teachers?

*Spiritual guides?

How to Consciously Make Relationship with Humans in the Inner Spheres
We Shape the World.

Let's return to our practice of visualization, as we did with Minerals, Plants and Animals. Visualize Your Finest Human Self, with this inspiration from Rudolf Steiner:

*In the free human being
The Universe gathers itself together.
Now, in the free resolve of your heart,
take yourself in hand,
and you will find the world.
The Spirit of the World, as well,*

will find Itself
in You.

- Let us again settle into our body. Allow our awareness to drift down from the head and settle more deeply into the region of the heart.
- Allow the breath to swing through the heart; you may feel that you are a child again, swinging in your back yard, from a long swing on the branch of a tree. Or perhaps you have an ancient memory of being rocked in a cradle.
- Be aware, in this movement, of how your breath enters and exits your being as pure gift. You need make no effort; life-giving breath simply arrives with fresh energy and buoys you up, lifting and filling not simply your lungs, but your whole being with the new.
- Turn your attention now to your heart, not the physical heart, rather to the subtle heart which exists in the central region above the solar plexus; feel the breath moving in and out of this center of love, this center of universal love.
- Feel your heart as a radiant source of warmth and light.
- Now gather into this radiant source of love your closest beloveds, family and friends. ----As you gather each of these beloveds, you will find that the space in your heart does not become more crowded. No...in fact your heart becomes greater and more luminous.
- Bring your entire community into this field of love.
- Bring in those you pray for: those in need, who sorrow, who suffer war, famine, flood.
- Bring in even those you find difficult; include them in the radiance of the One Heart.
- Now bring those you find impossible into the huge generosity of the Universal Heart.
- Bring our whole majestic, vulnerable, exquisite planet directly inside your vast heart.
- Now, holding all these beings, return to your breath swinging through your heart.

- Be aware of love and gratitude for this human life, with all its glory and sorrow.
- Now on your breath, arrive here, home, back in your body, in your heart, in your love.

Who are the people in your life that model this Finest Human Being for you? Whose heart is vast and holds love as the central force? Write about these beloved mentors in your Rewilding Journal.

Questions to Deepen These Relationships

- If they are alive and close: spend time with them. Learn through resonance by sharing in their heart rhythm.
- Whether living or not, present or distant: Bring them into your heart meditation each day and have inner conversations with them. Ask advice and offer thanks.
- A way to ask "what is it like to be you?" is to *slip inside their skin*, the way you slip inside the skin of your best beloved.
    a. Now, *feel* the gift they bring to you.
    b. Now intuit, from inside their skin, what gift you can offer them.
- Ask for their advice and help as you move toward sleep.

End with several breaths. *Offer Blessing to Air and Humans.* Commit to explore your relationship with Air and your human models more fully as you move through your days. Honor the air with your breath. Greet and give gratitude to your ancestors or teachers each day. As you walk through your day, keep them at your side; see the world through their eyes. Breathe in unison with them.

DEEPENING PRACTICES FOR CHAPTER FOUR

Again we will bring our learning into all aspects of our being: into our bodies, hearts and souls, as well as our minds. We will inform our bodies with action: giving care and attention to our

Place for Honoring the Realms, and our Gratitude Bundles. We will educate our heart and soul by collecting images and feelings and will give loving imagination to our Kinship Collage We will enrich our life of thought by mindfully attending to our internal inquiry questions recording them in our Rewilding Journal. All of these offer gratitude and blessings to Air and Humans.

PLACE FOR HONORING THE REALMS: OUTDOOR SIT-SPOT OR INDOOR NATURE PLACE

This week we will bring Air and Humans to join our honoring place that includes earth, minerals, water, plants, fire, and animals.

Air itself is not visible to us; we "see" air only in its effect: leaves rustling, clouds moving, fields undulating. Now you can bring objects that remind you of the invisible power of the Air Element. Perhaps you have found a meaningful feather, or collected maple seedpods and pressed autumn leaves? Light incense and meditate on the swirling smoke riding air currents. Each day we breathe air, given us by the benevolence of the trees; we attune to and breathe with all beings.

For this chapter we also bring to our altar photographs, ideas, words, poems, and works of art that connect us to our human teachers. We greet and honor them. We breathe-in the qualities of being they model for us and then breathe these gifts out into the world. We give honor and thanks for the qualities of spaciousness, interbeing, relationship, and communication. We bow and smile.

CREATE A GRATITUDE BUNDLE FOR THE AIR ELEMENT AND REALM OF HUMANS

Life creates the conditions necessary for life. By alchemy, ancient plants slowly changed Earth's gaseous atmosphere into Air that was breathable by reptiles, birds, mammals, and humans. Ancient trees generously changed carbon dioxide, water, and sunlight into sugars to feed themselves as well as to ~ happily ~ create oxygen for us to breathe. We call this process photosynthesis, and we are very familiar with this fundamental precept. Let's not take it for granted and remember that *Gift* is the principle of all Life. It is the gift of the Plant Realm that has made life possible for animals and humans to breathe.

Breath is the great unifier. We breathe air created by ancient trees, and each breath that enters our bodies has been breathed a hundred thousand times already by bobcats, orcas, grizzlies, blue-footed boobies, Amazonian tree frogs. Ancient cultures knew that thoughts, not human thoughts alone, are carried on the wind. We breathe this wisdom with each breath.

Let us learn to listen well, and to take guidance from our Elder-Beings. It is our human privilege and responsibility to give honor and thanks to the wise life force, and original instructions, that enter our beings with each breath. We do this by offering "Earth Prayers," our gratitude bundles for the nourishment of the Element of Air and the Realm of Humans.

- Again you can begin with either a piece of paper or a large leaf. If you choose paper, paint or color an image that represents the Air Element and Realm of Humans, or write a poem to honor them.

- Now you gather the items that go inside of your paper or leaf, to make the offering package. Fold in a way that honors earth, sky, generosity and encircling protection. Tie as before.

- We offer our bundle for the nourishment of the Air Element. I have done this in two ways, but perhaps you will think of other ways. I have taken my bundle and tied it into the branches of a favorite tree, a tree who is my friend and companion. Each day as I walk past, I greet the tree and bow with prayers of honor and gratitude. I have loved leaving the bundle in the tree throughout the changing seasons and also the changing years! It is lovely to witness the caress of wind, sun and rain....to honor the life-giving process of decomposition.

- Another way I have given this gift: After tying the bundle into a beloved tree, choose a number that is meaningful to you. When that number of days has passed, remove the bundle and ceremonially tear it into small pieces. Offer the pieces to the wind the way autumn leaves offer themselves.

+   You give away the bundle to nourish the Element of Air and the Human Realm.

Create your own prayer, or use the following as a spring board. Make your prayer audible, sing or speak, as you give the offering:

Oh, beloved Air, how do we even begin to give you thanks? It is through you, breath-of-life, that we are made kin to all beings, that we learn wisdom composed of the lives lived by all earthlings. They have breathed their journeys into the atmosphere that cycles abundantly about us. Help us to know the ways of Air as intimately as bird nations and cloud beings know. Let us remember you with each breath; let us waste no breath with forgetfulness. We give you honor, gratitude and love. Please accept this prayer bundle from my deep heart.

KINSHIP COLLAGE
Choose images that represent the *Air Element and Realm of Humans*. Create a collage that integrates these Air Beings and Human Beings into the unified whole that we experience as we walk breath by breath through our living earth.

REWILDING HUMAN NATURE JOURNAL
Record your work with the Questions for Inner Inquiry into your relationship with Air, as well as practices to deepen your kinship with our Human family.

CHAPTER FIVE

The Ether Element and Realm of Unseen Beings

We Are One ~ Vast Unity

IN THIS CHAPTER, we explore Ether as the integrative force ~ that miraculous gathering together of all Elements, Realms, and Beings into the coherent interdependent living being we call Gaia. We look within, as well, and make relationship with this integrative force within our body, heart, mind, soul, and spirit. We explore-into the world of Nature; with the eye of the heart we see and honor the Unseen Beings that are always teeming in the living atmosphere of our home, Mother Earth. We also turn our gaze inward toward the unseen Spirit Beings who nurture, guide and protect us. We give thanks and honor for the qualities of Oneness and Inter-Being.

Let's begin exploring the Element of Ether ~ the Integrating Force ~ with a different sort of story, this time with a suite of poems "To Honor All Beings."[37] After hearing this, we will *Breathe in communion with Ether.*

TO HONOR ALL BEINGS

Minerals

Minerals are stardust coalesced in deep space,
messengers of light shot from Sagittarius' bow.
Luminous arrows, they travel through
a new sun's orbit. Pulled by love's gravity
they shape the intelligence of light into
Appalachia's igneous core.

Woman-in-mountain is our sister

breasts twin peaks
waist a deep valley
hips rising smooth
long thigh bone
a treeless ridge.
Her minerals tumble through our blood
like stones carried in highland freshets
come to rest for a time
in our shoulder blades, our ribs,
then flow on to nourish sacred ground.

Water

Water Beings arrive as pure benediction.
Ice diamonds fall through interstellar space,
drift into earth's warm breath
to become mist hovering above
river's slow elbow. Translucent curtains of rain
billow in valley breezes.

Drops sipped from cupped hands
will flow differently now, eddying among veins,
osmosing cell walls, hydrating neural highways.
Particles of human thought will flow out
to soil organisms, migrate into Ivy Creek,
eager to find the sea. To be pummeled by surf,
pause in tidal pools before becoming
northern blue ice, an Inuit kayak paddling close.

Plant

Rivanna river bank's damp earth,
a fecund womb, gestates plant embryos
who dream of water
        grace fallen from stars

who ache toward sun's warmth
    his sovereign ascendency.

Plant ancestors live through our cycles
moon to moon
    blossoming, fruiting
    seeding, germinating, gestating.
We are kin to seductive honeysuckle,
    unfurling first leaves, opening
    blossom's fertile whorl into
    crimson dawn light.

Kin to masting beech trees ~ sisters, cousins ~
    who together as one launch their precious young,
    making forests fill with music: nuts cascading
    from upper stories, squirrels gathering,
    gossiping amid leaf litter

Kin to blackberry vines
    who open their taut, sweet fruit
    into lustrous solar face.

Animal

Wide cretaceous wingspan, heron descends
in majesty, steps high with ancient grace
through autumn's garden stream.

With a cool intense gaze she studies
creek-bank, stream bed,
plucks a crayfish midstream.
She is an elegant Asian woman
who reaches with chopsticks to extract
a plump water chestnut.

Woman moored at the window,
a slight quiver trembles between
shoulder blades as bird ascends,
cruising with slow deep wing beats.

Coyote prints in mud, bear scat amid birdseed
possum's marsupial parenthood:
we bow to animals' warm blood,
bequeathed to us through ancestry.
We salute the sun-being who walks across
his blue arch, raying out beneficence,
generosity, the gift of fire.
Our limbs are warm, hearts ablaze.
Free.

Light

Fire's incandescence dies into silk. Albedo. Ash.
Cool, nutritious, alabastrine as spider's web,
ash sweetens acid soil, warms with a tender hand:
    destruction becomes eclipsed by grace.

Ash, nutrient rich, dug back into human soil
    alkalizes, phosphorizes, bio-luminesces.
No longer making light by heat, we metamorphose.
Now our lucid prayers
    and conversations with glowing fungi
are coronas of light in the dazzling dark:
    we become the communion
    of light upon light.

Air

We grow translucent with imprint of wind.
Conjoined Spirit,
    composed of god's breath and

signatures of animal kin,
opens our gills-become-lungs.
Oxygen cycles through geologic time,
through an elongated history
of evolving bodies' animate tissue.

Breath is a tender sharing, honed through millennia
    coevolved with conifers, tree frogs,
    great blue heron, black bear mothers.
Vapor, breeze, gust, zephyr:
living air, lived inter-being.
To be a gnat in this amaranthine wind
    vanished inside the whirling
for a moment we are one photon
in the eye of god.

Human

We are composite, a permeable form
 the world-spirit travels through:
    minerals, waters, plants,
    animals, starfire, wind.
We welcome these guests,
    Spirit embedded in Earth.
We tend them as they flow through us,
know that elements borrowed
from star-born ancestors will be returned
for our children's children, thoughout generations.

Breathe in communion with Ether.
Now let's sit and hold the feelings these poems engender, as we breathe with the Unity of Being, which is Ether. Let us greet Ether with honor and gratitude.

    Beloved Creator Ether, I greet you with Gratitude and Love.
        Your Unity unites me with all beings.

Your Oneness is the One I live within.
You weave all beings into one unfolding continuity ~ Love.
Through you We are One.
 I give you honor and praise.

– Sit comfortably and relax, breathing in and out through the nose and the mouth, with lips slightly open.
– Enjoy a few breaths and relax into the rhythm.
– With each inhalation become aware of layers of integration: this is life itself.
– Your protons and neutrons are integrated to become the nucleus. Your electrons orbit the nucleus; this level of integration creates an atom.
– Atoms integrate together and evolve into a molecule.
– Be aware that your molecules become integrated into the cell.
– Feel your cells integrate to become tissues.
– Breath by breath zoom outward, into awareness of the integrative forces of your body. This is a miracle we may take for granted but can become ever more aware of.
– Breathe this miracle which is your body for a few minutes. Relax and enjoy the interior vastness.
– Now on the inhalation gather into your heart all your most beloved people. Be aware of the integrated "field of love" that you and they live within.
– On the exhalation allow your love to energize and amplify this field.
– Take a few breaths and be aware of the integration ~ the interbeing ~ you create together.
– Allow this integrated field of love to encompass those who are one circle beyond your center, beyond your family and friends. Let love encompass your community.
– Moving in concentric circles, allow the integrating force of love to extend as far as you are comfortable.
– Perhaps you can hold your watershed, your bio-region, your continent, our planet.

- Can your heart-breath open and be integrated with the entire Universe?
- When you are ready, on the exhalation allow your blessings of love and gratitude to mingle with the light of the stars.
- End with a deep bow of gratitude.

Ether in the Outer Landscape
We Are One

The awareness of Ether ~ Interbeing, Spirit, the Integrating Force ~ has been with humanity for millennia. The sense of Ether as an element was held by medieval alchemists, Greeks, Buddhists, Hindus, the Japanese, and the Tibetan Bon, each with their own understanding of its nature. This circles us back around to where we began this journey of reunion. In Chapter One, while exploring earth and minerals, we talked about the generative principles that have shaped and formed Gaia Herself. The spiritual forces of self-creation and self-maintenance lie invisibly behind and inform every interaction in the body of earth. Gaia is a unified conscious, intelligent Being. She is a holon within the holarchy of the cosmos. She is a super-organism nesting within the ever-greater superorganism of the cosmos.

Self-creating and self-maintaining: The following is from *Sacred Depths of Nature*, by Dr. Ursula Goodenough, who is not only a leading cell biologist, but among her many other accomplishments, she is the president of the *Institute on Religion in the Age of Science*. "The origin of life marks a momentous event: the origin of the self. We usually use the word self to refer to our experience of being a human person. But we can also use the word self to describe every organism, all the way back to earliest single-cell beings. Self-awareness does not have to be the criteria for selfhood. Each self is capable of doing self-directed work, is self-maintaining, self-protective and self-repairing."

We discussed holons earlier; remember that a holon is a whole "being" ~ a self ~ nested within interconnecting larger "selves." Holons are whole selves living within ever greater realms of whole selves. The whole selves that are electrons and protons are held nested within the larger self that is the atom. The atoms converge to become the molecule.

The molecule is held within the larger self ~ the cell. The cell is within the organ, the organ within the body, the body within the family, the community, the unnumbered ancestors, the vast entwined family of nature. All selves are held within the Universe. *The living evolving Self that is Spirit breathes through every manifest form.*

From the beginning, in their innate wisdom, earth-cultures have seen all beings as persons ~ as selves. Having been raised within the predominant western paradigm, it was only in my teens that I discovered this understanding of personhood bequeathed to all life. I was reading a book telling of adventures in Africa. The author referred to baboons as "the *people* who sit on their heels." This turned my world upside down; suddenly the tightly constrained walls of my human-centric worldview crumbled in one swoop. There before me, now, was spread an animate, breathing being, pulsing with selves ~ with people ~ each as intelligent and essential as I!

From the level of cells and molecules to ancient matriarchal societies, the care of these interdependent, ever-cycling, ever maintaining selves is of the foremost importance. This need for care is met by principles of abundance, distribution of resources according to need ~ not merit, by generosity, cooperation and collaboration, egalitarian decision-making, and culminates in gratitude and celebration. Not only is care of these intertwining lives essential, the care of their death and regeneration is essential, as well. Earth operates in a state of constant transformation and is the protector of essential life and death cycles. She is a great Self, protecting all the intercycling selves that make up her body. Earth is a vast composting system: forests, prairies, waters, oceans, migrating animals depositing nutrients in rhythmic cycles; bodies dying, decomposing, composting, and recomposing. All these dynamically interacting selves are the act of *Life creating the conditions necessary for life and are gifts of Ether ~the Integrative Force.*

All earth cultures also see self and land as indivisible. This is the unitive consciousness of Ether, and it affirms "We are the Land." What we have been exploring through these chapters is the sacred and indivisible bond between the Sacred Earth and our Sacred Self. This chapter by chapter, piece by piece study is reintegrated by immersion in the consciousness of Ether. We are the land, minerals, waters, plants, fire, animals, air, humans. We are the Ether and the Unseen Beings. Like all life we are an impermanent state of consciousness through which all these cycling, metamorphosing forces enter. They interact with us metabolically, emotionally, spiritually, then move swirling into further relationships. All these beings distribute blessings into our being; they then carry our blessings out into the world. When the one we call "I" dies, all these elements ~ these selves ~ that compose this "I-ness" continue their eternal journey of ever-living, ever-regenerating, ever-maintaining. We are One.

Ether in the Inner Landscape

The Ether Element in the inner landscape mirrors Ether in the exterior.[38]

The primary quality of Ether, or Spirit, is Unity. In the woodcut above we see Ouroboros, a gnostic and alchemical symbol that expresses the unity of all things, material and spiritual, which never disappear but perpetually change form in an eternal cycle of destruction and re-creation. This is not a monolithic or static unity, rather it is dynamic consonance which engenders a sense of communion and coherence. An orchestra, with its woodwinds, brass, percussion, strings and keyboard ~ each section so dramatically and specifically different from the others ~ creates harmony. Harmony is a state of unity within diversity.

Each of the following definitions of Unity reflects a different state of consciousness: "Unity is the quality or state of not being multiple." This is a very narrow definition that doesn't accommodate for this Unity within diversity. The following definition is a more comprehensive understanding of Unity: "A totality of related parts: an entity that is a complex or systematic whole."

"Ether is the beginning and the end; it is peace; it is the universal emptiness that is full and the fullness that is empty."[39] The Ether Element is so subtle, it often eludes the mind, which prefers its legion of words. I began to understand the Ether Element more fully when I took my meditation practice off the cushion and into the woods. This became an alchemical journey of transformation under the tutelage of my woodland relatives. While walking, I allow my footsteps to come into rhythm with the breath swinging through my heart. Tuning breath and footsteps together brings a grounded embodied state of awareness. Everything slows down. This offers the time needed to soften the gaze, widen the scope of vision, and breathe in communion with this wider field of love. Deepening into embodiment, the senses become open and receptive. With each inhalation we welcome in sight, scent, sound, touch and therefore the myriad person-beings who offer us these gifts. These mingle with the gift of our unique soul and are radiated out on the exhalation. Each breath unified with the nature-beings is a gift both given and received, then given again to the world. With each cycle of breath, we feel our consciousness expanding, welcoming and exploring. We feel the entirety of our integrated self being touched and touching our more-than-human relatives.

The following is a piece I wrote hoping to describe "catching" words that are alive and malleable enough to honor the unitive oneness of Ether.

MIND
"I am in the garden, listening for thoughts to be able to tell you what it is like. It's different than you imagine; not at all what we have been taught.

Spider teaches me to weave a web, a perfect geometry of proportion, symmetry and depth. It is spun of the substance of my own soul. I sit inside this translucent architecture and wait. Spider and I ~ old beyond time ~ we fish in the currents of earth's breath, the mind of Gaia. Our nets billow in life's breeze as shoals of thoughts, schools of ideas swim in their organic choreography of One.

We are designed to wait and breathe, to ride the currents of wind. Here is the breeze of a hummingbird's wing, and here the wind of sycamore's respiration. Words come floating by. I catch one, gaze and turn it over, sniff and taste. Is this a messenger true enough to slip through the barbarian's mine field, penetrate and disarm the weapons of mass distraction aimed at a twenty-first century mind? I wrap each word in silk, so, when strung together they will be prayer beads. I hand this living rosary to you. May each word-being open and its foliated perfume call to you: *Step out of the mausoleum of concepts and into the living mind of the forest."*

We can deepen and practice relationship to Ether in the inner landscape by using the breath in this way:

- Inhale "I am *within* the One Being." Feel all being-ness drawn into your very body, heart, soul. Feel the swirling dynamism settle into a calm, vast center point in the heart.
- Exhale "I am *united* with all beings." Feel beingness birthing, radiating, whirling out from this calm center, manifesting and becoming our exquisite earth.
- Stay with this until you can easily simplify the words to become
    *Inhale: "Within the One."
    *Exhale: "United with All."

There are many other practices to deepen relationship to Ether, as well. For me, breath ~ one of the technologies of relationship we began with ~ is the central touchstone and this is the reason we have consistently turned toward breath in these explorations. But it is your freedom to explore and discover *your own* "go-to consciousness expander." Other ways of weaving relationship and experiencing interbeing can be as creative as your own imaginative soul.

- Song can bring you to unitive experiences of spirit.
- Conscious movement, dance, and ritual open doors as well.
- Potent images that suggest to you the union of all beings can be portals to inner experience.
- Keep inspirational writings on the bedside table or at your desk; they can act like a gong of remembrance before falling asleep, or in the midst of a busy day. Read small fragments. Choose a phrase or image, then breathe the words on the inhalation and exhalation.

Unseen Beings in the Biosphere

Vast Unity

Within the boundless dancing whirl of earth-life, we humans have evolved the exact perceptual field designed to serve our human needs. We are now learning this is a very limited view. Many "unseen beings" are unseen by us simply because it is not necessary that we humans see them. Most species' senses are designed to give the essential information needed for their particular survival, and ours are the same.

Colors that are beyond what human sight and minds are equipped to see are present in the atmosphere. Yet animals and insects see these fluorescent colors because they are essential to their survival. David Attenborough's series *Life in Color*[40] is an amazing visual reminder of the Unseen Color-Beings. The same is true with sounds: bats, whales, dolphins, some shrews, hedgehogs, and a few birds hear by echolocation. Snakes don't have external ears, rather their inner ear connects to the jawbone, and when the sound waves vibrate, they "hear" through vibration.

We humans have developed tools that help our gaze go further and deeper than the naked eye; they allow us to see some of the infinite realms of Unseen Beings. Telescopes and satellites let us see a small sliver of the unseen cosmos. Microscopes let us see the miraculous communities of Unseen Beings that live inside our own bodies, as well as those of soils, plants, animals, microbes, slime molds and more. LIDAR imaging helps geologists see under the earth's surface, to discover ancient sites and uncover unseen pasts.

Societies can choose to either encourage or discourage aspects of the perceptual field. A friend of mine told of an experience he had while working as a health care giver within an aboriginal Australian community. His work was to go into the communities to help support their health and well-being. He would visit with a client, then make an appointment to check in again the following week. A week later he would arrive to discover his client was nowhere in sight. He would then begin searching through the village, asking of their whereabouts. Sometimes it took an hour to track them down, or worse, the appointment would be missed altogether. One of these frustrating days, in his search, he asked a villager's help. Although the neighbor did not know the client's whereabouts, he did ask, "Why do you waste all this time running around?" My friend replied, "But I need to follow-up with them. What else can I do?" The neighbor, completely mystified by such naiveté, said, "Well, just sit down and *think* about them!" He went and sat under a tree where he visualized his client, who then appeared in front of him in short order! This story points toward western culture's narrowing of the perceptual field, yet most earth cultures continue to recognize and make relationship with Unseen Beings.

Unseen beings of light within Christianity are called Angels and their hierarchies are many. Other cultures call beings of light by other names: in East India they are called Devas; within the Hebrew tradition, they are Shedim; Egyptians name them Afries; for Persians they are called Devs. Originating in Greece and continuing within European earth cultures, elemental beings are recognized as the "spirit" of the physical phenomena and are called gnomes, undines, sylphs, and salamanders. Plant Spirits are recognized as teachers and healers by most traditions world-wide. Spirit animals acting as guides for humans appear in nearly all traditions.[41] Dream Beings are not visible in this world, but they can powerfully guide us throughout an entire lifetime. Ancestors are recognized around the world as consistent sources of wisdom

How to Consciously Make Relationship with Unseen Beings in the Inner Spheres

There are many gifts in making relationship with the realms of Unseen Beings. They can be our guides, companions, healers, comforters, supporters, teachers, confidants. Let's return to our practice of visualization. Let us greet the Unseen Beings:

Beloved Unseen Beings,
Your presence is palpable amid our human days.
Your shimmer glistens at the corner of our eyes.
Your whispers guide us in our dreams.
Your inspirations enlighten our words and deeds.
We give you Gratitude and Love.

    — Let us again settle into our body. Allow our awareness to drift down from the head and settle more deeply into the region of the heart.

    — Allow the breath to swing through the heart; you may feel that you are a child again, swinging in your back yard, from a long swing on the branch of a tree. Or perhaps you have an ancient memory of being rocked in a cradle.

    — Be aware, in this movement, of the way your breath enters and exits your being as pure gift. You need make no effort; life-giving breath simply arrives with fresh energy and buoys you up, lifting and filling not simply your lungs, but your whole being with the new.

    — Widen your attention and become aware of the Unseen Beings that always accompany us. Do you feel the presence of your ancestors? The Spirt of Earth, Water, Fire or Air? Perhaps you are aware of the ethereal presence of your angel. Maybe you feel the palpable presence of your spiritual lineage. Or a plant or animal guide? Who consistently accompanies you? Who comes to you in time of need?

    — Make an open invitation: is there an unseen being in your life who is asking to go deeper now? If you receive no answer, ask again tomorrow. Keep inviting.

    — When your invitation is accepted, you can
        *Light a candle daily. Sit with them and listen.
        *In time, ask questions
            What gifts do you bring me today?

What do you ask of me today?
Ask for guidance with your difficulties.
*Invite them into your daily life, keep them close
beside you as you go about being human.

End with several breaths. *Offer Blessing to Ether and the Unseen Beings.*
Commit to explore your relationship with Ether and the Unseen Beings
more fully as you move through your days. Honor the Ether with your
breath. Greet and give gratitude to the Unseen Beings. As you walk
through your day, keep them at your side; experience the world from
within the field of love that is Interbeing. Breathe in unison with All.

DEEPENING PRACTICES FOR CHAPTER FIVE

Remember Ritual: Our bodies are designed to learn through
action. *Action* is the way our *body* understands life, and therefore
we learn <u>what to do</u>: Give care and attention to your Honoring
Space and Gratitude Bundles. *Images* are the way our *heart*
understands emotion and therefore we learn <u>how to feel</u>: give
loving imagination to your Kinship Collage. *Thought* is the way
our *mind* understands (both analyzing and synthesizing experiences) and therefore we learn <u>how to respond</u> to life: mindfully
attend to your internal inquiry questions and your Rewilding
Journal. All of these offer gratitude and blessings to Ether and
the Unseen Beings.

PLACE FOR HONORING THE REALMS: OUTDOOR
SIT-SPOT OR INDOOR NATURE SPACE

This chapter we will bring to our altar the Ether Element and the
Realm of Unseen Beings. They join our Earth, Minerals, Water,
Plants, Fire, Animals, Air, and Humans.

Ether is the unifying force, the intelligence of the One Being
which holds all life on Earth and in the Cosmos, in wholeness
and harmony. Now let's bring to our altar objects that remind
us of the unifying power of the Ether Element. For me, images

from the Webb Telescope portray this universal force. Perhaps you have other images: the whorl of hair on a newborn's head, the spiral of a nautilus shell? Or perhaps you contemplate the Fibonacci Sequence or the Julia Set?

Be sure to see the resources listed in the Appendix to find images for your honoring space, as well as zoom sequences to illuminate your mind. Let's attune to our honoring space and find within it keys to the intelligence of the Universe. We can also bring images, ideas, words, poems, and works of art that connect us to our spirit guides. We greet and honor them.

We give gratitude to the integrative force of Oneness: to all beings, seen and unseen.

REWILDING HUMAN NATURE JOURNAL
Record your work with the Questions for Inner Inquiry into your relationship with Ether, as well as practices to deepen your kinship with Unseen Beings.

CREATE A KINSHIP COLLAGE
We live and experience our being within the integrative miracle that is the Element of Ether. In the preceding chapters, we have slowly deepened into our primal relationships with:

The abundant gifts of Earth and Minerals.

The life-giving womb of mother Water and her allies the Plant Realm.

The inspiration and enthusiasm of Fire, as well as the warmth of our Animal cousins.

The collective wisdom that enters our humanness as Air.

Now we live into the miraculous gathering-together of all these, our relatives, as they live within the Earth and ourselves. We see this integrated Dance of Life whirling about us in deep woods, on city streets, in pristine grasslands, classrooms, streambeds, hospitals, farms, hidden beaches, and in crowds of people. It is through the Eye of the Heart that we witness and participate in this living miracle. Allow your Kinship Collage to hold this warmth and intelligence.

AS WE END, WE WILL MAKE OUR GRATITUDE OFFERING DIFFERENTLY

Now, after you have created your collage, rather than giving it away to the Elements and Beings, hold it in your sacred place, where you will see it often. It is a road map to bring you home again and again to your own *Rewilded Human Heart.* You "give it away" differently now. You nourish life by remembering that you walk through the world with your Sacred Self imbedded eternally within the Sacred Earth. You live in joyous co-creation with all beings.

A final Prayer of Gratitude and Remembrance
These lines are from a poem by our national poet laureate Joy Harjo. Allow it to resonate in your life as a sacred prayer:
Remember

Remember the plants, trees, animal life who all have their
tribes, their families, their histories, too. Talk to them,
listen to them. They are alive poems.
Remember the wind. Remember her voice. She knows the
origin of this universe.

Remember.[42]

Appendix

Heartfulness Meditation

This is a meditation I have been practicing for nearly forty years. Much to my surprise, I discovered about fifteen years ago that the Heart Math Institute, www.HeartMath.org, not only teaches a very similar meditation but has done hundreds of research studies that validate the physical, emotional, social, and cognitive benefits of a simple heart-based meditation. Most significant to this technique is *to know that a positive feeling is more important than trying to empty the mind of thoughts.* To care for our self and feel the *goodness* in our own heart is the essential nugget. This equanimity then spills over into all aspects of life.

It is easiest to begin when you have a bit of quiet time, to get the felt experience of its simplicity. It is designed to be practiced, though, with eyes open and in the midst of a busy life.

LET'S BEGIN

1.) In the Western world, we usually experience consciousness as located in our heads. Allow your consciousness to slowly drift down and settle, resting, in your heart. This is not necessarily the physical heart but rather the heart center, in the central area of your chest. You can rest your hand on this central area, if it helps you to *feel* your awareness relaxing in your heart.

2.) As you simply notice this heart area, you will become aware of your breath moving through your lungs. This movement of the breath very subtly "rocks" you. Feel your body slightly sway, as though you are in a hammock being rocked by the breeze.

3.) Allow yourself to experience this movement as peaceful, positive. I call this feeling "goodness". Other positive emotions may also arise such as appreciation, harmony, well-being, sometimes love. Gratitude is a natural doorway to love. If these emotions do not arise naturally, you can remember a person or an occasion in which you felt this goodness. Focus on the *feeling*, not the memory.

4.) Now you remain with the felt experience of the breath moving through your heart. Perhaps like me, you will focus on this micro-movement through your whole body and feel the goodness this brings. This heart-breathing is a first step toward self-compassion.

5.) As thoughts, emotions, and sensation arise, bring these experiences into the peaceful resonance of this heart-space. Don't follow their "storyline," just allow them to be gently rocked in your heart. There is room for all of life in this heart-expanding meditation. If emotions other than goodness arise, such as sorrow, anxiety or anger, you can also bring these into your heart-space. Within the coherence of the heart, you can allow the breath to move through these negative emotions, as well. Observe and see what effect your rhythmic breath and open heart bring.

6.) Another option is to do this meditation with eyes open while standing and slightly swaying side to side. This emphasizes the calming quality of rhythmic movement.

When we regulate and "steady" the heart's electromagnetic field through meditative practice, perhaps while walking in nature, the heart's powerful "field of resonance" brings all our physiological systems into harmony and balance. All systems become entrained to the coherence of the heart. Our own state of coherence then brings others we encounter into resonance as well.

Follow this link, and join me in the Heartfulness Meditation https://www.youtube.com/watch?v=6nr63KQzZrY

Rewilding Resources

Chapter One: Earth and Minerals

The PBS series Native *America: Explore the world created by America's First Peoples.* This video series features original mound-building societies and illustrates their deep embeddedness in the Element of Earth. The four-part series reaches back 15,000 years to reveal massive cities aligned to the stars, unique systems of science and spirituality, and one hundred million people connected by social networks spanning two continents.

Kiss the Ground is a beautiful, accessible documentary that walks us through the healing aspects of regenerative agriculture. Healing the soil will heal the planet. https://kissthegroundmovie.com
   And here is the link to the Kiss the Ground Organization: https://kisstheground.com

Soul Fire Farm and Leah Penniman demonstrate for us the healing not only of the land (and *fast* carbon re-sequestration) through regenerative agriculture, but also the empowerment of BIPOC folks through food sovereignty. This farm is amazing! https://www.soulfirefarm.org

Biodynamic Agriculture: Farming in Service of Life
   This short video about biodynamic farming will open your heart-mind and inspire your relationship to the soil. It's too beautiful to miss: https://youtu.be/yyO9SyeO4ww

Cave of Forgotten Dreams studies a 36,000-year-old cave in France, filled with exquisite Paleolithic depictions of animals, landscapes and the presence of humans. As I watched this, I was stunned by the glittering crystalline blanket that moves like silk across the walls. Watching this is to experience life in a crystal cave. https://www.amazon.com/Cave-Forgotten-Dreams-Werner-Herzog/dp/B005EPFA8I

Heart Meditation: Follow this link to a video in which I teach a very simple open eye, open heart meditation that can be done anywhere at any time. I love most to do this as a walking meditation, moving consciously and with an open heart through the woods. Try it; if you stay with it, it will change your whole life: https://youtu. be/6nr63KQzZrY It is sustenance for any hunger, shelter from any storm, rest for the weary, beauty to balance human ugliness, courage to continue to step forward and so much more.

Chapter Two: Water and Plants

Water Stories. Zach Weiss offers us this beautiful website. He and his team demonstrate how we can heal the water cycle through low-tech earthen water-catchment systems. In this simple way we bring life back to desertifying lands. He offers trainings in this and other systems, to heal the water cycle. https://www.waterstories. com/about

Snail Girl Brings Water is a beautiful Navajo story that tells us much about ourselves, Navajo worldviews, and also about the sacred nature of water. I always love to learn origin stories, as a way to understand the consciousness of the people I am drawn toward. https://www.amazon.com/Snail-Girl-Brings-Water-

The Water of Life, by Llewellyn Vaughan-Lee. If you are not familiar with Emergence Magazine yet, now is the moment to dive in! This is from the editors: "It has always been a radical act to share stories during dark times. They are regenerative spaces of creation and renewal. As we experience a loss of sacred connection to the earth, we share stories that explore the timeless connections between ecology, culture, and spirituality. In a landscape where nothing is certain and old patterns of control tighten their grip, Llewellyn Vaughan-Lee urges us to leave behind that which no longer nourishes us and work with the Earth toward a living future." https://emergencemagazine.org/op_ed/the-water-of-life/

Diana Beresford Kroeger is a world-renowned scientist who was taught the ancient Celtic wisdom of trees as a child. She was told one day she would need to bring this knowledge to the world. That time is now. She says, "The wisdom of the past is the key to earth's future." Also, "Rebuilding the global forest is the cheapest and best defense against climate change." Follow this link to her website and scroll around until you find her conversation with Jane Fonda on Fire Drill Fridays. https://dianaberesford-kroeger.com

Chapter Three: Fire and Animals

The Indigenous practice of Good Fire is an excellent article on the use of "good fire," and how California is partnering with local tribes. It is good to read deeply into the article, to discover the difference between Indigenous cultural burns and Forest Service prescribed burns. "Cultural burning comes back to *what we are burning for,* and it's not burning for acres," Goode says. "We're burning to restore the land, restore the resources, restore water. Bring it back to where it can reproduce on its own." Cultural burning, in other words, is for the nurturing of relationship!
https://www.universityofcalifornia.edu/news/how-indigenous-practice-good-fire-can-help-our-forests-thrive

More on Indigenous burns: "However, the authors argue that these programs (prescribed burns) risk simplifying Indigenous methods into a small set of tools that have an easily measured impact on greenhouse gas emissions. Instead, they write, truly community-based solutions must go hand-in-hand with protecting and reviving Indigenous communities and increasing their control over their own traditional territories."
https://daily.jstor.org/the-global-suppression-of-indigenous-fire-management/

Native Skywatchers Initiative seeks to remember and revitalize indigenous star and earth knowledge. The overarching goal of *Native Skywatchers* is to communicate the knowledge that indigenous people traditionally practiced a sustainable way of living and sustainable engineering through a living and participatory relationship with the above and below: sky and earth. https://www.nativeskywatchers.com/index.html

Obama's "Our Great National Parks" This is a Do Not Miss; see all five episodes! These are worldwide national parks in which we see footage of animals from the entire globe. We see them in family groups, gathering food, caring for, playing, hunting, making alliances and friendships with other species. The best glimpse into the "more-ness" of the more than human world! https://www.netflix.com/title/81086133

Deepening our Relationship with Fire: Here you find one of my YouTube videos about fire. https://youtu.be/eI4yIUQ3Lvw And another of mine with fire stories: https://youtu.be/UXByl2ddU0s

Chapter Four: Air and Humans

Assembly of First Nations website: "Air is a life-giving force and necessary for survival. The Element of Air stands for the life force that brings all people into existence from their first breath. The ancient ones have long understood that the wind is the intermediary plain which connects the spirit world to our own. Air also symbolizes the mental and spiritual process which brings understanding and inspiration through thought and form." For more exploration: https://www.afn.ca/honoring-air/

Environmental Protection Agency, Actions You Can Take to Reduce Air Pollution, https://www3.epa.gov/region1/airquality/reducepollution.html

California Air Resources Board, Fifty Simple Solutions to Help Reduce Air Pollution, Sept 19, 2011. https://ww2.arb.ca.gov/resources/fact-sheets/simple-solutions-help-reduce-air-pollution

Chapter Five: Ether and Unseen Beings

Here we find links to images and ideas that portray the miraculous Multiplicity Within Unity that we call the Universe, or Spirit.

Images from the Webb Telescope. Peruse these images and be mind-blown. Perhaps bring the most potent and powerful to your Honoring Place.
    https://www.google.com/search?q=images+from+the+webb+telescope&client=safari&rls=en&source=lnms&tbm=isch&sa=X&ved=2ahUKEwiqis3hpKf8AhVzg3IEHa_lDOsQ_AUoAXoECAEQAw&biw=1440&bih=752&dpr=1

The Fibonacci Sequence in Nature:
    https://www.google.com/search?q=Fibonacci+sequence+in+nature&client=safari&rls=en&source=lnms&tbm=isch&sa=X&ved=2ahUKEwiF34f_r6f8AhXM-FVkFHSqLC8QQ_AUoAXoECAEQAw&biw=1440&bih=752&dpr=1

The Mandelbrot Set: From Wikipedia about fractals: "The Mandelbrot set has become popular outside mathematics both for its aesthetic appeal and as an example of a complex structure arising from the application of simple rules. It is one of the best-known examples of mathematical visualization, mathematical beauty, and motif." This link takes you to a TED talk by Benoit Mandelbrot, discussing his amazing work with Fractals:
    https://www.youtube.com/watch?v=ay8OMOsf6AQ

Look at the Julia Set; it is so beautiful and melodic: https://www.google.com/search?client=safari&rls=en&q=julia+set+zoom&ie=UTF-8&oe=UTF-8#fpstate=ive&vld=cid:53147d5a,vid:YOneAeBz8BQ

Joy Harjo's poem "Remember":
https://docs.google.com/document/d/114zM16YFckXsJPwkapQBQ-aNt-SuOWyqK/edit?usp=sharing&ouid=105303493084497009638&rtpof=true&sd=true

The Native Self Versus the Myth of the Autonomous Being: This article is a clear and concise elucidation of a Native sense of self as compared to non-native: https://www.se.edu/native-american/wp-content/uploads/sites/49/2019/09/A-NAS-2017-Proceedings-Csaki.pdf

Notes

¹ This image appears in Mary Oliver's poem "Wild Geese," in New and Selected Poems, Volume One, which won the National Book Award, 1992.

² A holon is something that is simultaneously a whole in and of itself, as well as part of a larger whole.

³ Emergence Magazine, Nov 5, 2020, Skywoman Falling. In this excerpt from the new introduction to her acclaimed book Braiding Sweetgrass, Robin Wall Kimmerer draws upon the creation story Skywoman Falling and the wisdom of plants to guide us through our present moment of deep uncertainty. The general arc of the story is true to Kimmerer's original; details are supplied by Sharifa. https://emergencemagazine.org/op_ed/skywoman-falling/

⁴ Each elemental breath and meditation is inspired by the work of the Sufi Master Hazrat Inayat Khan.

⁵ These salutations are inspired by my friend Christopher Moinuddin Clarke

⁶ This "creation image" is from the Webb Telescope and in public domain.

⁷ In each chapter we will take a small sip from the fountain of alchemical wisdom offered by Carl Jung, with much gratitude to my Spiritual Guidance teacher Thomas Atum O'Kane.

⁸ Many thanks to Llewellyn Vaughan Lee for the gift of this story, so many years ago!

⁹ Be sure to check the Resources Section for Zach Weis's Water Stories. There you will find wonderful graphics that bring forth the aliveness of the water cycle.

¹⁰ Hassett, Fisher, Money, "Mushrooms as Rainmakers," NIH National Library of Medicine, Published online October 2015. Accessed July 2023. https://www.ncbi.nlm.nih.gov/pmc/articles/PMC4624964/

¹¹ Zach Weiss

¹² Diana B Kroeger: see below.

¹³ 15 Chrysalis of Apatura clyton (Emperors) from Moths and butterflies of the United States (1900) by Sherman F. Denton (1856-1937). Digitally enhanced from our own publication. Free download under CC Attribution (CC BY 4.0). Please credit the artist and rawpixel.com.

¹⁴ From John O'Donohue's book of poems To Bless the Space Between Us. https://

bookshop.org/p/books/to-bless-the-space-between-us-a-book-of-blessings-john-o-donohue/8667514?ean=9780385522274

[15] https://www.ncbi.nlm.nih.gov/pmc/articles/PMC3887317/. Martins Ekor, published online January 2014.

[16] Diana Beresford Kroeger, The Tyee, Dec 31, 2020, https://thetyee.ca/News/2020/12/31/Tree-Scientist-Seeks-Nature-Well-Being-Pandemic/

[17] Eleven Ways Plants Enhance Your Mental and Emotional Health," Susan McQuillan, Psychology Today, 9-14-2019

[18] Ruth Kirk, Tradition and Change in the Northwest Coast: The Makah, Nuu-chah-nulth, Southern Kwakiutl and Nuxalk. Seattle: University of Washington, 1986.

[19] This story is mentioned in Calvin L Martin's The Way of the Human Being, Yale University Press, New Haven, 1999, Chapter "...to the Skin of the World." It is fleshed out and retold by Sharifa.

[20] David Abram, "Creaturely Migrations on a Breathing Planet," Emergence Magazine, June 8, 2023, https://emergencemagazine.org/essay/creaturely-migrations-breathing-planet/?utm_source=Emergence+Magazine&utm_campaign=11d84bdf45-

[21] www.nativeskywatchers.com

[22] Lyla June, "3000-year-old solutions to modern problems," TEDx Talks, September 29, 2022, https://www.youtube.com/watch?v=eH5zJxQETl4

[23] Salamander in Flames, Michael Maier, Atalanta Fugiens, first published 1617. In public domain.

[24] Many thanks, again, to Moinuddin Clarke, for these inspiring words.

[25] Natural History Museum, James Ashworth, July 20, 2022. https://www.nhm.ac.uk/discover/news/2022/july/mammal-ancestors-became-warm-blooded-burst-late-triassic-evolution.html#

[26] Mulvihill, Conor, "How Animals Shaped the Evolution of Humans," Green News, May 6, 2016. https://greennews.ie/how-animals-shaped-the-evolution-of-humans/#:~:text=One%20of%20the%20earliest%20defining,for%20language%20developed%20more%20recently.

[27] Organization of Nature Evolutionaries offers Earth Rights, Earth Writes, and Earth Rites. This website is a Do Not Miss! https://www.natureevolutionaries.com/earth-rites

[28] This traditional Japanese tale is retold by Sharifa Oppenheimer. You simply must click this link to hear the story told beautifully by Odds Bodkin and accompanied by a Celtic harp! https://www.oddsbodkin.net/shop/crane-wife-stories-love/

[29] For an overview of Schauberger's revolutionary study of water, scroll down to "The Magic and Majesty of Water" by Callum Coates. https://www.alivewater.com/viktor-schauberger

[30] You must watch this! The power of speech is portrayed in this short film, The Lindworm, produced by Emergence Magazine. Master story-teller Martin Shaw retells this teaching tale. https://www.youtube.com/watch?v=z7-uZSIUSpU

[31] United States Environmental Protection Agency, https://www.epa.gov/clean-air-act-overview/clean-air-act-title-iv-noise-pollution#:~:text=Health%20Effects,sleep%20disruption%2C%20and%20lost%20productivity.

[32] Spirit of Air, Michael Maier, Atalanta Fugiens, first published 1617, in Public Domain.

[33] https://www.mindandlife.org/insight/why-we-need-indigenous-wisdom/

[34] 36 Donahue, Glasser, Preuss, Van Essen, "Quantitative assessment of prefrontal cortex in humans relative to nonhuman primates" PNAS, May 2018. https://www.pnas.org/doi/10.1073/pnas.1721653115#:~:text=Many%20studies%20have%20reported%20that,primates%20(10–16).

[35] Dr. Heidi Abendroth is the "mother of matriarchal studies." Her work is revolutionary! https://www.goettner-abendroth.de/en/matriarchy/

[36] You must read The Dawn of Everything, by David Greaber amd David Wengrow, October 2021, Penguin Books. https://en.wikipedia.org/wiki/The_Dawn_of_Everything

[37] These poems are reprinted from A Litany Of Wild Graces, Sharifa Oppenheimer, by permission of Red Elixir Press.

[38] Spirit of Union, Michael Maier, Atalanta Fugiens, first published 1617, in Public Domain. Ouroboros is a gnostic and alchemical symbol that expresses the unity of all things, material and spiritual, which never disappear but perpetually change form in an eternal cycle of destruction and re-creation.

[39] Again, thanks to Moinuddin Clarke for this classic definition of Ether.

[40] See David Attenborough's Life in Color. https://www.youtube.com/watch?v=SwexvE91lRI

[41] Mark Boyer's book An Abecedarian of Animal Spirit Guides: Spiritual Growth through Reflections on Creatures, looks at animal spirits in world religions.

[42] "Remember," 1983 by Joy Harjo from She Had Some Horses. https://www.joyharjo.com/book/she-had-some-horses

Sharifa Oppenheimer was the founding teacher of the Charlottesville Waldorf School and is the author of numerous parenting books including the well-received *Heaven on Earth: A Handbook for Parents of Young Children* and *With Star in Their Eyes: Brain Science and Your Child's Journey Toward the Self*. After writing extensively from her experience, wisdom and love of young children, she has turned her hand toward writing about other aspects of profound connection. In new book *Rewilding the Human Heart ~ A Journey of Reunion*, she invites the reader to travel with her into a new and ancient relationship with the living earth. She strips away of the veneer of "nature appreciation" and guides us toward a home-coming celebration of humanity's primordial embodied symbiosis with Gaia. Trekking through the outer terrain of the cardinal elements with her brings us into a deepened understanding of our own beating heart. *Rewilding the Human Heart* is a companion to her recent book *A Litany of Wild Graces: Meditations on Sacred Ecology* in which she expresses ~ through essays, poetry, and dreams ~ humanity's biological and spiritual inter-being with our other-than-human relations.

Visit her website *Wild Graces*
https://www.sharifaoppenheimer.org
And her Substack Rewilding the Human Heart
https://sharifaoppenheimer.substack.com

www.ingramcontent.com/pod-product-compliance
Lightning Source LLC
Chambersburg PA
CBHW031521270326
41930CB00006B/462